Having Faith in Foreign

HE Anthony Bailey, KCSS, Gautam Banerji, The Rt Hon John Battle MP, Rabbi Tony Bayfield, The Rt Rev and Rt Hon Lord Carey of Clifton, The Rt Rev Lord Harries of Pentregarth, Sunny Hundal, Urmee Khan, Sadiq Khan MP, Daleep Mukarji, The Rt Rev Bishop Dr Michael Nazir-Ali, Richard Stone, Daniel Wheatley

Edited by Alex Bigham

HAVING FAITH IN FOREIGN POLICY
Editor: Alex Bigham

First published in 2007 by
The Foreign Policy Centre
Suite 14, Second Floor
23-28 Penn Street
London N1 5DL
UNITED KINGDOM
Email: info@fpc.org.uk
© Foreign Policy Centre 2007
All rights reserved

ISBN-13: 978-1-905833-09-2
ISBN-10: 1-905833-09-1

Acknowledgments

The Foreign Policy Centre is indebted to a number of people for their help with this report.

They include the contributors: HE Anthony Bailey, KCSS, Gautam Banerji, The Rt Hon John Battle MP, Rabbi Tony Bayfield, The Rt Rev and Rt Hon Lord Carey of Clifton, The Rt Rev Lord Harries of Pentregarth, Sunny Hundal, Urmee Khan, Sadiq Khan MP, Daleep Mukarji, The Rt Rev Bishop Dr Michael Nazir-Ali, Richard Stone, Daniel Wheatley, There are many other people who assisted in various ways including Anil Bhanot, Diane Fisher, Barney Leith, Charles Reed, Dr Austen Ivereigh and Stephen Twigg. We are grateful to all of them.

This report would not have been possible without the generous support of HE Anthony Bailey, KCSS, and Eligo International (www.eligo.net). We also record our thanks to the Grand Magistral Delegation for Inter-Religious Relations of the Sacred Military Constantinian Order of Saint George (www.constantinian.com).

Cover design by Alex Bigham, © 2007.

Disclaimer
The views expressed in this report are not necessarily those of The Foreign Policy Centre.

Preface

Alex Bigham

The task of encompassing the diverse religious and faith communities in Britain is immense. This report is not intended to be a representation of the spectrum of faith opinion in the UK, but rather a collection of viewpoints from faith leaders and thinkers who attempt to answer some of the most vexed questions of our age: what is the relationship between religion and the state in a post-modern society; what is the interaction between faith, conflict and development and how can governments and leaders reach out to citizens who may feel disengaged from foreign policy?

Religion and faith have played a valuable role in the history of humanity, promoting social justice, challenging tyranny and providing cohesion. But religion has also been used as an ideology to justify conflicts and oppression.

Fundamentalism of all strands is still worryingly present – some claim it is on the increase. It is a misguided and sometimes bigoted reaction not just to modernity, but also to tradition. The challenge of defeating such an ideology lies not with one particular religion, but with society as a whole.

There are many interfaith, single faith, and cross-community groups, who have done immense work to stand up to such fundamentalism. But most would agree that this can never be enough – the challenge is to reach out to the wider community, to build a progressive consensus, which shows, as one of our contributors puts it, – that liberal religion has more in common with liberal secularism than it does with fundamentalism.

The first six chapters of this report encompass some of the broad challenges, opportunities and concerns of faith leaders and intellectuals when facing a globalised world which is in continuous flux. They consider the historical contexts of both theological and political debates, the roots of conflicts – both religious and secular, and outline some tentative steps for reform.

The second half of the pamphlet features six essays focussed on specific issues but which still have universal relevance – military intervention; Israel/Palestine; the war on terror; human rights; the Muslim veil; and international development.

Two messages stand out in this collection. One is that the very process of informed engagement between communities and individuals – what John Rawls might have called the process of civic toleration provides a roadmap for better relations. The second is that however strongly felt the differences are between faiths, religions and cultures – and the associated intellectual tradition of relativism, there are some truths we hold to be universal: the freedom of speech, the freedom of belief and protection from persecution, to name but three.

Alex Bigham is the Communications Officer of the Foreign Policy Centre.

Contents

Foreword by Lord Carey of Clifton

1. **Faith and Diplomacy**
   John Battle MP   9

2. **The Role of Religion in Society and the World**
   Bishop Michael Nazir-Ali   14

3. **The Jewish Experience in Britain**
   Rabbi Tony Bayfield   28

4. **A Clash of Civilisations - the Paradox of Globalisation?**
   Sadiq Khan MP   48

5. **Religion and British Foreign Policy**
   Gautam Banerji   56

6. **How do we tell the real story?**
   HE Anthony Bailey, KCSS   61

7. **Military Intervention from a Christian Perspective**
   Lord Harries of Pentregarth   70

8. **Impact of Israel/Palestine on UK Muslim-Jewish relations**
   Richard Stone   74

9. **The War on terror – not just an issue for Muslims**
   Sunny Hundal   83

10. **Faith, Human Rights and the Question of Universalism**
    Daniel Wheatley   89

11. **Defrocking Muslim Women**
    Urmee Khan   96

12. **Religion, Development and Foreign Policy**
    Daleep Mukarji   102

Foreword

Lord Carey of Clifton

That our world is in great peril few would doubt. Some might think swiftly of issues to do with the environment and global warming, others will focus on soaring population growth which has plunged two thirds of human beings into absolute poverty. Serious though these are, the peril of religious fundamentalism is also dire and dangerous. The problem is that adherents of religious fundamentalism claim such authority and sovereignty for their own beliefs that terror and violence become acceptable options to achieve what they believe to be the will of the God.

In the chapters that follow senior religious leaders and experts dig deep into the causes of disputes among religions and the widespread and troubling cultural clashes that are currently disfiguring our planet. Their conclusions echo many of mine honed through years of debate with leaders of other faiths, as well as from close working with them. I am convinced that all faiths and religions must face up to the challenge of modernity. Those who appeal for the exclusivity of their faith (that mine is wholly right and all others are wholly false) must reckon on fierce questioning, however certain they may be of that opinion. Those who believe their scriptures are infallible and, consequently, that their laws should take priority over civil law, will be rightly challenged and expected to justify that opinion.

However dangerous and difficult our situation today clearly is, a new opportunity for dialogue has arisen as moderates within all faiths have protested that intolerance, bigotry and terrorism should not be allowed to define religion. I had the honour when I was Archbishop of Canterbury to host with the Prime Minister of the United Kingdom, Tony Blair, the first International Dialogue between Christian and Islamic scholars. This engagement at a scholarly level continues, and is replicated in many places throughout the world. I am delighted to note that since 9-11 a new conversation among the faiths is proceeding by way of hospitality, discussion and friendship and not as a dialogue of the deaf, or, even worse, as a form of megaphone diplomacy.

Of course, the scholarly issues are not the only ones that matter, and often, are not always the most important. Great grievances exist between religions and between the communities that they represent. Muslims sometimes complain that western governments are unfair in their treatment of Arab nations, when compared with preferential treatment given to Israel. Whilst acknowledging the technological superiority of the West, Muslims often condemn what they believe to be its moral decadence. From the other side, grievances are often expressed about Islamic countries – that human rights are frequently transgressed, that women are treated shabbily and that the Christian faith, and other non-Muslim faiths are discriminated against in Muslim lands.

However, none of these grievances and opinions is of such nature that it is beyond resolution. The way to resolve them is exemplified in this collection of essays. It will always be courtesy, respect, fair argument and face to face discussion that will help create the better world we all seek. 'Jaw-jaw, not war-war' was Winston Churchill's jocular remark made before the Second World War. Perilous times can only be averted when we apply the loving principles implicit in all our faiths to the challenges of a world that is most desperately in need of faith that builds up – not religion that destroys.

The Rt Rev and Rt Hon Lord Carey of Clifton, is the Co-Chair of the Council of 100 of the World Economic Forum, Chairman of the Foundation for Reconciliation and Relief in the Middle East and Chairman of the World Faiths Development Dialogue. He was Archbishop of Canterbury from 1991 to 2002.

Faith and Diplomacy

John Battle MP

A rough scanning of the major twentieth-century wars and conflicts would seem to prove right Marx and Freud's prediction of the declining influence of religion, especially in Europe. Religious beliefs were not the causal spark of the major world wars or the raising of the Iron Curtain. Following the fall of the Berlin Wall in 1989, and a de facto – and premature – declaration by some American commentators of a total victory by the remaining 'superpower', the debate on the future of religion, certainly in Europe and America, refocused around Darwin, the science of evolution and the development of the enlightenment – until the attack on the Twin Towers on 9th November 2001, which brought the wider world of Islamic beliefs into sharper focus, and a renewed discussion of Samuel Huntingdon's crude 'clash of civilizations' thesis.

The Roman Catholic theologian Eduardo Mendietta[1] insists on a wider perspective. Acknowledging that worldwide religious dynamics have accompanied contemporary economic and political events, he suggests that "with the break-up of the Communist governments of Eastern Europe and the Soviet Union, former smouldering religious embers have erupted into prairie fires interconnected with national, racial ethnic territorial and linguistic wars [...]" The destabilising of the geopolitical configuration caused by the collapse of the Berlin Wall and the effects of having a single world superpower have produced regional disputes often clothed in religious language. In other words, like ruffles in a newly-laid carpet, efforts to iron out immediate problems re-emerge further along the room as residual conflicts, arbitrary boundaries and ethnic and tribal differences resurface in an instantly accessible globalised world. Localised, deep-rooted historical differences re-emerge, as the current 44 serious conflicts around the globe make explicit,

---

[1] E Mendietta, 'Religions/Globalization', 2001

whether it is in Christian-Muslim conflicts in the Moluccas islands of Indonesia, or the Arab-African conflicts in Darfur, Sudan. In the new twenty-first century interconnected world, the local is now global. Moreover migration amplifies the impact of local conflicts, so that with increasing urbanisation the local conflicts of the entire world can be replicated cheek by jowl, in the tower blocks and terraces of our 'global cities'. Tackling international conflicts is therefore as much a local matter as action to achieve consensus at the UN Security Council.

In my constituency of inner-city Leeds, two men I know of, who had moved to Leeds from India and Pakistan respectively, walked down the street where they both lived without speaking to one another for twenty-three years. Between them was the conflict over Kashmir, caught in the redrawing of the boundaries between India and Pakistan by a Labour Government in 1948. For both of them it remained a much neglected, unresolved and violent conflict. But following the catastrophic earthquake in October 2005, they were seen returning from the paper shop arm in arm. I asked what had got them together. The man from Pakistan replied, "I saw an Indian truck on television taking tents and blankets into the earthquake victims of Azad Kashmir, so we've decided to call off the war in our street. For this is where we live now and where we'll die." The tragic earthquake and the collective community responses had brought them together.

Mendietta is positive in reminding us that, "For the majority of cultures around the world, religion thoroughly permeates and decisively affects the everyday rituals of survival and hope. Reflected in diverse spiritual customs, sacred symbols and indigenous worship styles, global religions are permanent constituents of human life. In fact for most of the world's peoples, religion helps to construct the public realm". Sociologically, of course, he is right, for most of the world's peoples in South America, Africa, Asia and indeed North America, the major global religions of Christianity, Islam, Hinduism, Sikhism, Buddhist and Judaism, are 'permanent constituents of human life', and, as Mendietta insists, "religious spirituality remains both endemic to controversy and empowering for social transformation, helping to refabricate new communities."[2] He points out that, "In the 'Third World' or 'Two-Thirds World' and in many minority communities, we find some of the clearest representations of a spirituality of resistance and positive social amelioration. The growing pressures of a global economy – energised by further squeezing by the World Bank, the International Monetary Fund, US monopoly corporations and local elites – have fostered a persistent resurgence of indigenous grassroots communities, often bolstered by liberation theologies and a politicised spirituality of survival and hope."[3] In other words, religion still matters, and in the early twenty-first century we are witnessing, not fewer, but a greater number of religious movements worldwide.

Britain, despite being officially a religious 'Church of England' state, is remarkably culturally post-religious, as the popularity of Richard Dawkin's *The God Delusion* would seem to show. The ferocious privatising of religion, 'keep it to yourself' approach, has led not to a retreat but to a renewed controversy of the role of religions in the public space. While the philosopher AC Grayling proclaims that "What we are witnessing is not the resurgence of religion but its death throes"[4] the reality, particularly in urban areas, is of the major religions on the ground actually providing a wide range of social and personal support services. The 'faith communities' recently recognised by national and local government are increasingly turned to as part of the solution to the challenges of social exclusion, rather than regarded as the problem, or being dismissed as in irrelevant terminal decline. Christian churches, mosques, gurdwaras, temples and synagogues, have been and are significant local service providers. What this implies is that there is no way of avoiding opening up a discussion of the nature of the relationship between faith communities and the state at local and national levels, between 'private' religious practice and actively living in the 'public square'. Renegotiating 'faith' and 'state' relations can no

---

[2]   Ibid.
[3]   Ibid.
[4]   AC Grayling, 'Against All Gods', 2007

longer be dismissed as an irrelevant issue, as increasingly through the globe 'faith communities' re-assert their right to their principles and practice.

Inter-faith cooperation, therefore, is not an option for beleaguered communities under threat of extinction, it is rather about exploring capacities for diversity through cooperation and dialogue – and at local and global levels. Developing a mutually acceptable 'modus vivendi' that enables believers and practitioners of different and even opposing traditions, to live together, cheek by jowl and cooperating on civic duties and responsibilities, ranging from supportive local social work to participation in municipal and national political activity to shape society's budgets and laws, is emerging as the twenty-first century challenge. There is a need to deepen dialogue beyond superficial 'get-togethers', to broaden the basic knowledge and understanding of the full range of differing religious traditions and practices (including differences *within* particular faith communities), and of course to engage the young, not only as participants, but to define the dialogue and to reshape agendas in the public space.

Perhaps the contemplative Christian monk, St Benedict, father of Western monasticism, should be allowed to set the tone with the opening word of his 'Rule': 'Listen', remembering with the contemporary Irish poet Michael O'Siadhail, that 'the opposite of love is not hate, but fear'. A climate of fear, fostered by an insistence on a war against 'terrorism', provides the most difficult of all circumstances in which to promote 'listening' to the other, but reaching out to deepen understanding and to open up new space for cooperation and shared vision has to be rooted in a new diplomacy of openness and risk. The assassinated Bishop of Oran, Pierre Claverie, who was killed by Islamic fundamentalists in 1996, was renowned for his understanding of Islam. He remarked in his final sermon: "I have come to the personal conviction that humanity is only plural. As soon as we start claiming to possess the truth or to speak in the name of humanity we fall into totalitarianism. No one possesses the truth;

each of us is searching for it". That search should include religious and non-religious alike.

The Rt Hon John Battle MP is the Member of Parliament for Leeds West and the Prime Minister's Envoy to the Faith Communities. He is a member of the International Development Select Committee and Chair of the All Party Parliamentary group on Overseas Development.

The Role of Religion in Society and the World

Bishop Dr Michael Nazir-Ali

More and more scientific research says that religious awareness or a spiritual sense is innate in human beings. It is not something acquired. It is not a virus with which people are infected from outside but it is something deeply wired into the human psyche. Work with children, for instance, is also showing that children have an innate spirituality, which is often driven out of them by grown-up attitudes.

Of course, religion is a very personal matter. It points us personally to what is beyond us to the transcendent. But it also has a social dimension. For many societies, religion provides the glue that sticks people together in particular communities and that it often lies at the root of many of our laws, our institutions and our values whether that is acknowledged or not.

But, many religious traditions also have a prophetic aspect to them. The ability to criticise social structures and to allow social renewal at critical times in history. Particularly, I think Judaism, Christianity and Islam can be singled out in this way, that there is an aspect of each of these traditions that can relate to society as it is in a way that is critical and that makes for social renewal. It allows for instance the poor to organise themselves against the powerful and for individuals to raise their voices against what they may see as injustice. Nor is this aspect limited to the Semitic traditions. The origins of Buddhism and Sikhism can be said to lie in a social criticism of caste and Hinduism itself had movements of this kind within it.

Of course we all know that religion can go horribly wrong. I have seen how religion has linked up with chauvinistic forms of nationalism. At the height of the Bosnian conflict, I went on behalf of Christian Aid to see how Christian Aid and Islamic Relief were working together in Bosnia and it was quite clear that some forms of religion had become the veneer for a very nasty kind of chauvinistic nationalism. Nowadays we are aware of the way in which religion, particular kinds of religion, have got associated with terrorist activity.

If religion goes wrong, then it is not unique in that sense because there are other basic aspects of the human condition which also go wrong. Love between people can go wrong. Many of us have experience of that. We all know how patriotism, love of one's nation, can become excessive and excluding. Even entrepreneurial flair can go wrong and result in the exploitation of people rather than in a good stewardship of creation. So it shouldn't surprise us that spiritual awareness or religion can also from time to time go wrong.

However, if we think of the many great injustices and cruelties that have been committed in the 20th century, then secularism cannot claim to be exempt from at least the charge that it is responsible for some enormities in our world. National Socialism was a secular ideology, so was Stalinism, so was the Maoist Cultural Revolution. These movements caused great suffering, as did Pol Pot in Cambodia. We have seen how the Baath party, a secular party, created so much suffering in Iraq. Religion doesn't have any monopoly on cruelty, exploitation, or oppression.

Both Christianity and Islam are world religions. They are both missionary religions, traditions that are growing rapidly in different parts of the world. They have both separately and together a responsibility not only for peacekeeping but also for peace making and we have to ask what each tradition can do in these terms. There is accountability for each. And they have to ask each other what they are doing in terms of peacekeeping and peace making.

A Historical Overview

There was never a time in history when Christians and Muslims were not living together, talking to one another, having to relate to one another. Along with Judaism, that is something quite unique to Muslim/Christian relations. The Prophet of Islam from the earliest days was aware of a Christian presence in Arabia. In trading missions he came across Christians in countries like Syria. Indeed it was in those countries that Islamic tradition claims his mission was first recognised. So Islamic tradition will name two monks called Bahira and Nestur who were supposed to have recognised that there was something special about the Prophet of Islam even before he began his work. His wife Khadija, who had been his employer seemed to have Christian relatives and there is a record of them and their interaction with Muhammad the Prophet of Islam and their influence indeed on him. All the time that Khadija was alive their marriage was monogamous, and some have taken that to mean that she had a Christian background.

When the Prophet began his mission in Mecca it was strenuously opposed by the pagan Meccans because they were engaged in a cult of the so called daughters of Allah – Allat, Al-Manat and Al-'Uzza – and Mohammad's preaching of Monotheism, of the oneness of Allah, who could not have daughters was opposed by them rather like the Ephesians opposed the preaching of St Paul because it threatened the cult of Artemis of the Ephesians.

When persecution became unbearable for the early followers of the Prophet, he remained in Mecca, but sent his followers into exile as refugees into the Christian areas of Abyssinia and Ethiopia, where they were received by immigration officials who interrogated them, as refugees are even today. But the interrogation was rather different from what might happen today. It was theological interrogation. The Negus, the ruler of Ethiopia, and his officials wanted to know what these people believed about Jesus and Mary. And the Muslims said that they believed that Jesus was a Word from God and a Spirit from him and that he had been born of a virgin. This appeared to satisfy the Ethiopian officials and they were given refuge on that basis. This act of hospitality by a Christian people has a place of great honour in the Muslim story, the early Muslim story.

When Mohammad went to Medina and acquired temporal power, there was considerable tension between the Muslims and Jewish tribes and certain unpleasant things happened to some of the Jewish tribes, which we must in all honesty record. But he promulgated the Constitution of Medina in which the rights and duties of all the different religious communities were recognised and they were placed on an equal footing. So that was the first Islamic state and when Muslims say to me that they want to have an Islamic state, I often say to them is it going to be like the Constitution of Medina, the first, the most primitive example of an Islamic state? This arrangement did not last very long for a whole number of very complex reasons but that it was attempted at all is remarkable.

Mohammad concluded treaties with both Jews and Christians in many different ways. When the Christians of Najran came to visit him, he accommodated them in the mosque of the Prophet in Medina, where of course Christians are not allowed these days on pain of death. But they were allowed to offer their prayers there and there was again a theological dialogue, and on that basis a treaty was concluded. The Christian of Najran asked the Prophet of Islam what he believed about Jesus. And again Mohammad said that he believed that Jesus was a word from God and a spirit from him. And the Christians then said, "is he the Son of God?", to which of course the Prophet replied "no", having opposed the cult of the daughters of Allah he could hardly now say that Allah had a son after all! We need to understand the Muslim denial of the sonship of Christ in its historical context. So the Christians of Najran said, "Well whose son is he then?

The Koran gives two answers. The first is that Jesus is the son of Mary. So what was in Jewish Christian polemic, a title that was used as an insult about Jesus was turned by Islam into a title of honour. Jesus, the Messiah, the son of Mary is said about Jesus again and again in the Koran. Secondly, the Koran asks Christians a counter question – whose son was Adam? And the answer that is given is that just as God created Adam out of nothing so by his creative word he created Jesus in Mary's womb, out of nothing. *Kun-fa-yakūnū* – be and it was, it says, a formula that Muslims often use to speak of God's creative power (3: 59 cf 4: 171, 19: 35).

The point that I am trying to make about the Prophet of Islam's relationship with Jews and Christians in the context of peninsular Arabia, is that during his lifetime, these communities were tolerated and indeed treaties were concluded with them.

After the death of the prophet, Islam spread more rapidly outside Arabia into what was then the Christian Middle East. It spread into Syria, Egypt, Palestine, Mesopotamia and began to knock at the doors of Byzantium. The Persian Empire, which was the other great superpower to Byzantium, fell very quickly. Many of the great cities were surrendered to the Muslims peacefully. The gates of Damascus were opened for the Muslim armies by the family Al-Mansūr – the family of the one who was later to become St John of Damascus. The Melkite governor in Egypt surrendered, and the gates of Jerusalem were opened by the patriarch Sophronius who invited the Caliph Umar to pray in the Church of the Holy Sepulchre. Omar declined to do so saying that if he did the Muslims would use this as an excuse to turn the Church of the Holy Sepulchre into a mosque. So he went outside and prayed. And of course if you have been to the Holy City, you will remember that the mosque of Umar is built on the spot where he is supposed to have prayed.

Although many of these countries and cities surrendered to the Muslim armies there was, in those early days, sometimes without the knowledge of the Caliph, the destruction of Jewish and Christian communities. They were expelled on the basis of a prophetic tradition that Arabia should have only one faith. It's a tradition that I regard as dubious because the prophet himself never did anything like that during his lifetime. There was also gradually a system of structural discrimination that was put in place. When the Muslim armies arrived in predominantly Christian countries, which also had Jewish populations, they had to rely on their subjects for much administration, and even some judicial work. So the codes of Justinian and Theodosius were taken over almost wholesale by the Islamic system simply so that daily affairs could carry on.

These codes influenced subsequent developments. The structured discrimination took various forms, which you can still see reflected in many Muslim countries. For example, a Muslim man could marry Christian or Jewish women, but Christian or Jewish men could not marry Muslim women. Eventually a system was established which is called the *Dhimma* – a word which means "responsibility", which meant that the Muslims would protect the Christians and the Jews, later on the Zoroastrians, and later on even people of other faiths, as long as they did not claim equality with Muslims and they accepted certain kinds of civil disabilities that were imposed. For instance they had to wear a special kind of dress, they could not ride on horses but had to ride on donkeys, they had to give way to Muslims, they had to pay a special tax, their houses could not be higher than Muslim houses, their churches could be maintained and repaired with the permission of the Muslim ruler but no new churches or synagogues could be built and so forth. This system of the *Dhimma* survived up to the 19th century. And it was largely because of this dispersal and discrimination that the Christian majorities of countries like Egypt and Syria were gradually reduced to minorities.

The interesting thing about the *Dhimma* is that it is both an advance and a problem. It is an advance because it tolerated people of another faith within the Islamic polity at a time when this was not usually the case. It was not the case in Western Europe, for instance. In that sense it was a genuine advance. But it was also a problem because it institutionalised discrimination against certain groups of people. There were certainly outbreaks of persecution from time to time and it removed groups of people from decision-making and from government for centuries. However, if we look at the *Dhimma* we also have to look at the development of the Islamic empire. Not under the first dynasty of caliphs the Ummayad dynasty, but certainly under the second dynasty, the Abbasids, the Islamic empire flowered into a very great civilisation.

There were two great disruptions to this civilisation. The Mongols who invaded the Middle East and Europe from Central Asia and, of course, the Crusades which began as a response to the actions of Seljuk Turks in the lands of the Bible. The Crusades were an attempt, initially, at containing the *Seljuks* and opening up access to the Holy Land for pilgrims. Those who suffered most, however, when the original aim was lost were the Eastern Christians. Nor were the Crusades directed solely at Muslims. There were Crusades against the Jews, Western heretics, like the Albigenses and against the city of Constantinople.

Eventually the Arabs lost primacy in the Muslim world and they were replaced by various groups of Turkish rulers – the last of which were the Ottomans who established the great Ottoman Empire. Under the Ottoman Empire the *Dhimmi* system of protected peoples, was refined to its finest point so different denominations of Christians, of Jews, of other religions, almost became nations within the empire and were treated like that. To do this, the Ottomans used the old Persian idea of the *millet*, or recognised community, which had been developed in relation to the Church of the East in the Persian territories before the Advent of Islam.

In the 19th century growing western relations with the Ottoman Empire – military and commercial – started to put pressure on the Ottomans to modify and eventually abolish the *Dhimma*. Through successive edicts of the Caliph in the middle of the 19th century, minorities, at least in theory, were given equal rights with Muslims. By the early part of the 20th century in the Arab world because of these edicts and, to some extent, dissatisfaction with Ottoman rule, a nascent nationalism emerged - the *Nahda*, or period of renewal. For the first time Christian Arabs played a significant role in the re-emergence/renewal of a sense of Arabness among the Arabs. In the early 20th century, the number of Arab Christians was much greater than it is now, They played a very significant part and if you look at the history of political parties in Egypt, in Iraq in Syria you will see that they had many

Christian leaders and even founders such as Michel Aflak, the founder of the Baath party.

So Arab nationalism accepted theoretically and intellectually the edicts of the Ottoman caliphs. It accepted that people were to be citizens in the new Arab states regardless of religion. The creation of Israel and the exodus of Jews from Arab countries meant that this was now restricted very much to Christians and Muslims. But up until 1948 the Jews were a major part of the scene. Some 20% of the population of Baghdad was Jewish until 1948. Although it has to be said that, because of the emergence of Zionism in the west, Jews of the Islamic world did not contribute to nationalism in the way the Christians did. It wasn't just Arab nationalism, but other kinds of nationalism also emerged, including Turkish nationalism and Indian Muslim nationalism.

To each of these nationalisms, Christians made a signal contribution. If you think of the constitutions of Islamic states that were written in the 1940s, 50s and 60s, you will find that Christian jurists like Chief Justice AR Cornelius of Pakistan made a signal contribution to the emergence of Muslims states. This is a paradox but nevertheless true. Cornelius, a devout Roman Catholic, described his work as that of a 'constitutional muslim' because he recognised that Islam had a role to play in the development of Jurisprudence in Pakistan.

So what happened then? Why did Arab nationalism recede into the background? What happened in Pakistan from the great vision of Mohammad Ali Jinnah, to a state that became to some extent theocratic?

Many reasons can be given for the return to Islamism, or the turning to Islamism, to the view that Islam could provide all the answers for polity, for the economy, for living together.

The first is undoubtedly the experience of colonialism. People felt increasingly that Muslim nationalist leaders had learned their various ideologies during the period of colonialism and that they were not home grown, they were not Muslim in inspiration and they were an exotic plant in Muslim soil. This experience of colonialism was reinforced by the experience of neo-colonialism. Many will remember what happened at the time of Suez, which Muslims understand as an experience of neo-colonialism. When a moderately socialist government was elected in Iran in the 1950s this was destabilised by Western powers because it wouldn't give them oil concessions. The Islamic Revolution of 1978 and 79 reaped the harvest of the removal of Prime Minister Mossadegh – a secular socialist leader – and the installation of the Shah in his place.

Neo-colonialism also surfaced later in Afghanistan where western interests armed, trained and financed different kinds of very extreme Muslim groups to ensure that Afghanistan became the Vietnam of the Soviet Union. Almost every terrorist movement now in the Muslim world has its origins and inspiration in the killing fields of Afghanistan in the 1980s.

Islamism was a reaction to colonialism and neo-colonialism, but also the corruption of the Muslim élite. If you read the work of 19th and 20th century Islamic reformers, such as Jamāluddīn Afghānī, they certainly rail against the West the colonial situation. But they give almost equal time to condemning the corruption of their own leaders. And today many Islamist movements, not necessarily extremist at all, will focus on how Muslim countries have been ruined by the excesses of their own leadership.

There was a failure of both Command Economy Socialism on the one hand and of Capitalism on the other in the Muslim world. Command Economy Socialism, which still survives in some places, resulted in inefficiency, corruption, a lack of goods in shops, it made the poor poorer and even the rich became poorer in some situations! Capitalism, where it was tried in countries like Iran and Pakistan, made the rich richer but the poor poorer. The revolution in Iran started in the slums of South Tehran, much improved since the revolution, but still you can see what it might have been like. And it moved from South Tehran to North Tehran where the Shah was trying to build a kind of Switzerland which was forbidden to the slum dwellers. I believe these are the main reasons why people moved from nationalistic ideologies to Islamist solutions.

Contemporary Issues

The first question that nearly every country is facing is the relationship between religion and the state. The answer that some Islamist movements are giving is that the relationship is one of coercion – the state and Muslims living in it need to be coerced into being fully Islamic. However, there are many Muslims who see that this is not the way. I was in dialogue with the former Chief Justice of the Supreme Court in Pakistan. He says the role of Islam in Pakistan is not to impose an Islamic state, but to persuade Muslims in following the way of Islam. I have no difficulty with that. But whether it is coercion or whether it is influence is a key question in terms of the relationship of religion to state – and not just in the Muslim context. This is also relevant in Britain, Europe and, in a different way, in the USA.

The question of theocracy is always around the corner in Muslim contexts but I have to say that whenever movements in the Muslim world have advocated theocracy, they have been very quickly marginalised. The Kharijites – the people on the outside, the people who were expelled – were the classic theocrats. *La hukm illa lillahi* – No rule but that of God alone. But they were never mainstream. Mainstream Islam has always had intermediate institutions. The Caliphate itself is an intermediate institution, the judiciary, the Sūfī orders and many other examples can be given in the religious, political and social spheres of civil society in the Islamic milieu.

Another issue in this area has to do with government by consent. I use that term advisedly, because the term "democracy" is a loaded word and it is my fear that some people will try to impose forms of democracy that have originated in other contexts on Muslim countries and they will once again be seen as exotic and will not take root and actually will cause further disruption and disturbance.

In many Muslim contexts, there are customs and traditions of government by consent. I was very pleased when in Afghanistan there was no attempt to impose Western forms of democracy but the *Loya Jirga* - which is not particularly Islamic but a traditional way of gathering people together - was used, after modification, so that, for example women could participate in it. Similarly in Iraq I hope that the temptation to introduce American democracy where everybody is elected from the person who takes your refuse away to the local Judge, that temptation is resisted and that Arab customs of *Shūra* (consultation), of *bai^{c}a* (of acknowledging leadership) are used to develop local forms of government by consent varying from one place to the other, of course. In countries that have experienced Ottoman rule it is particularly important to notice the history of autonomy which countries have and to develop forms of governance which recognise this reality.

How religion relates to law-making is another important question in many parts of the world. Many codes of conduct, such as the Ten Commandments, have emerged from religious traditions and continue to influence the legal traditions of nations. The relationship of *Shari^{c}a* to law is especially prominent today and there is much misunderstanding. How does *Shari^{c}a* as divine law, relate to *fiqh* or its legal codification and what are the possibilities of development in *fiqh* and in new approaches to *Shari^{c}a* through *Ijtihād* and the concept of *maslaha* or the common good? Now some Islamist movements claim that the *Shari^{c}a* is given, that you cannot change it in any way, it cannot develop. This is quite wrong, because in three of the four main *Sunni* schools of law there are principles of movement in the *Shari^{c}a*, which allow the jurist to engage with the context, and in each school there is a different way of doing it. This is also the case in Shiite Islam. I was talking to some senior ^{c}*ulama* in Iran some time ago and they said that the relationship between revelation and reason is crucial for Shiism, especially in relating *Shari^{c}a* to contexts. Even the school, dominant in Saudi Arabia, which is supposed not to allow any taking into account of context has been shown by scholars to have some possibilities of movement within it.

Another very big question in Muslim/Christian relations has to be on the justifiability of conflict in the context of international order, the need to keep peace. Christians are used to the "Just War" theory, as some have applied to the conflict in Iraq. But Just War theory now has to be adjusted to new kinds of conflict which are emerging because they are not war in the formal sense. In Muslim/Christian dialogue we need to bring about an engagement between Just War Theory as Christians have held it and the Islamic idea of *Jihād*.

I said this once to some American officials, and they said "Oh Bishop, we know what *Jihād* is we don't need you to tell us". I think it is very dangerous for the West to misunderstand the concept of *Jihād* which is a very broadly based one in Muslim tradition. The word comes from the root verb *"jahada"* which means to make an effort. And one expression of it *ijtihād* is used by jurists precisely to relate law to context. But the word *jihād* is also used in many other senses. The *sūfīs* – the Islamic mystics – use it in terms of overcoming the lower self so that the higher self, the spiritual self, has control over the lower self. In the case of armed conflict *jihād* quite often means the permissibility of conflict when Islam is in danger.

In the 19th century when some Wahhābī movements wanted to wage *jihād* against the British in India, many Muslim leaders like Sir Syed Ahmad Khan, said "no, you can't wage war against the British because Islam is not in danger". In effect, that put an end to Wahhābism in British India. It is worth understanding what *jihād* is, under what conditions conflict can take place for a Muslim and to engage with Christian ideas of Just War so there is at least some convergence about when armed intervention, say for the sake of peace keeping or combating terrorism, might be permissible.

There is then the question of reciprocity, a word that we hear quite often. Reciprocity for me does not mean tit-for-tat. It doesn't mean because Muslims can have a mosque in Sydney therefore Christians must have a church in Riyadh. It really means that Muslims and Christians together should be committed to respect basic human freedoms of expression, of worship, of speech wherever they are and whenever they have influence. That will, indeed, raise questions about freedom of worship, belief and change of belief in every context.

Finally, there is the relationship of poverty to terrorism. This is not a straightforward matter but it is hugely important. It is certainly true that many of the leaders of terrorist movements are not from the poor. They are either from a wealthy background or at the very least they have acquired technological expertise. So they are educated people. But they *use* the poor to further their aims. This is certainly the case with Al-Qaeda, it is the case with the Taliban that poor children, whose parents could not send them to ordinary schools were sent to the *madrassas* in Pakistan and Afghanistan, were radicalised by people who did have the resources and who put the resources to work in these thousands of religious schools. In spite of attempts to check these tendencies, radicalisation is still going on in many of the *madrassas*.

So fiscal reform in Pakistan, for example, which President Musharraf began, but has now run aground to some extent, was very important because without fiscal reform a state can never provide the infrastructure to help the poor. Education – government regulation of the *madrassas* is vital, and again there has been some partial success in that area but the widening of the syllabus, making sure that people are aware of what is going on in the rest of the world, is being resisted by the leadership of these schools.

Alongside reform of the education system, it is extremely important for people to be able to have the skills required for a decent job and have resources available for entrepreneurship. It is here that the work of micro-finance is so important. We need to give people the means to earn their bread, perhaps to employ one or two people and it is from this, that there will be a genuine challenge to the kind of poverty that is such a breeding ground for extremist movements of all kinds. I urge micro-finance organisations not to forsake the Muslim world because things are difficult. We should not just be looking for short-term gains, for reports that read well and reassure our supporters. What we need is a faithful, committed and long-term presence. It is that which will make a difference.

Spiritual awareness is very much part of our make-up and religion has provided the cohesion but also the prophetic critique which societies need. I have admitted, however, that religion can go wrong just as other important areas of human life can.

I have focussed on Islam and Christianity as the two great universal faiths which have a responsibility for peace in our world. I have looked at the long and varied history of their interaction and have tried to learn some lessons about our world today. The Westphalian consensus is dead. The genie is out of the bottle. For the foreseeable future, religion will play an important part in the ordering of society and in determining relations between peoples and nations. It is our duty to see that such a role is benign and draws upon the best in each tradition. Whether that happens is largely up to the leaders, scholars and faithful of these traditions. Let us pray that it will.

The Rt Rev Dr Michael J Nazir-Ali is the Bishop of Rochester. A member of the House of Lords since 1999, he holds both Pakistani and British citizenship. He has studied, researched and taught at a number of universities and colleges in different parts of the world.

The Jewish Experience in Britain

Rabbi Tony Bayfield

Using the Particular to open up a Wider Discussion

There are a number of debates which arouse Jewish sensitivities. One centres on whether the *Shoah* (Holocaust)[5] is unique. Leaving aside the standard argument (the only instance of a large scale, technologically-based attempt to exterminate a whole people for no reason other than it existed), major historical episodes form a unique part of a people's story (we 'hug' them as 'ours' alone). But they also have echoes and parallels in other people's stories. This can make the event **both** *sui generis* and paradigmatic at the same time - that is, with direct relevance not just to the Jewish community, but with wider implications for us all.

It is with that observation in mind that this paper will reflect upon the history of the Jews in Britain. Since no two events are identical and contexts change, one must be very careful not to overplay the paradigmatic. It is easily done both by Jews and in relation to Jews, since that is the role Jews have played (held ourselves out as playing? been cast in?) for more than 3,000 years. At the same time, it is axiomatic as far as Jews are concerned that history is revelatory and a fundamental source of learning.

British Jewish History in Four Episodes

1656 and all that
Tiny numbers of Jews came to Britain with William the Conqueror, settled here, made lives, experienced anti-

---

[5] The very terminology is contentious. Holocaust means a burnt offering and carries Christian overtones of sacrifice. Jews prefer the term *Shoah* (catastrophe, destruction) arguing that Jews were not burnt offerings, they were simply burnt.

Semitism,[26] were exploited and then expelled in 1290 by Edward I. This was the first of the major European expulsions of the Middle Ages.

The return, in 1656 under Cromwell, is shrouded in mystery with pages deleted from the Council minute book. What began then was an aspiration that has been almost universally characteristic of Jews in Britain over the last 350 years. Namely, a desire to be able to practice Judaism openly and freely whilst, at the same time, living as fully contributing equals in wider society.[7] We can describe this as *seeking integration without assimilation.* The period since the Jewish resettlement in Britain is characterised by small groups of Jews establishing communities (centred on synagogues) so as to have the necessary content, structures and interactions to perpetuate Jewish life whilst, at the same time, pursuing many of the same social, cultural, economic and political ambitions as their Christian neighbours. Both integration (desirable) and assimilation (undesirable)[8] are supported by the ethnic similarity between Jews and their hosts.

1881-1905

This is the period of the major influx of Jews into this country – from Eastern Europe (100-150,000). The newcomers were to bring about significant change in the character of the Jewish community. They came from Poland, Russia and Galicia. They sought refuge from violent persecution – *pogroms.* They were also economic migrants fleeing, for instance, the intentional economic effects of the contraction of the Pale of Settlement and

---

[6] In one instance, the sad story of William of Norwich (1144), England actually originated the blood libel which is still alive and well and doing its diabolic rounds in countries like Saudi Arabia. The blood libel, prevalent at Easter time, accuses Jews of murdering Christian children and using their blood for the Passover ritual.

[7] The possible exception, that of the distinctive Hasidic and Haredi communities of Stamford Hill, Gateshead and now Golders Green, Hendon and Edgware, is of post-Second World War origins and should be seen in the context of the rise of fundamentalism since the 1960s (see section 2.4).

[8] My value judgement!

of desperate poverty in Galicia, then part of the Austro-Hungarian Empire.

The new immigrants were, in the main, extremely poor and distinctly 'foreign'. Significant, sometimes violent, tensions emerged between them and the local population – for instance in the East End of London. It is truly cautionary to read, for example, in Chapter 3 of "East End Jewish Radicals" by William Fishman[9] – of the full extent of the negative reaction to the newcomers. Indeed, the introduction of the Aliens Act in 1905, a watershed in British history, has a very unsavoury background. It brought about a rapid diminution in Jewish immigration and flashes up that word paradigmatic in neon lights.

The Jewish immigrants from Eastern Europe brought with them certain skills. Amongst these were tailoring, cabinet making and shoe making. These required little capital expenditure beyond a sewing machine or last – and little command of English. What emerged was a generation which, not without exploitation by their co-religionists, managed to make a living, put down roots and produce children who moved onwards and upwards. A deep cultural valuing of education, the widespread availability of public schooling, a strong drive to get on – and few alternatives – enabled many of the children to progress into the professions and up the economic and social ladder, buying into the values of British society, joining the middle classes and eventually enjoying life in suburban villas in the company of significant numbers of their co-religionists.

I want to avoid making this sound like a mass journey from immigrant poverty to Thatcher's Finchley in a couple of boot-strapping steps. Many of the immigrants brought with them from Eastern Europe socialist and bundist traditions which echoed the provisions of the Torah and had real connections with the demands of the Hebrew Prophets for social justice.[10] Jews found

---

[9] Duckworth, 1975.

[10] Forty years ago, I bought a book entitled The Socialist Tradition: Moses to Lenin by Alexander Gray (Longmans, 1946).

enthusiastic places not just in business and the law but in the political system – soon becoming significantly over-represented in the Labour party – in the universities and in the caring professions. There was clearly a sympathetic relationship between Jews and Judaism on the one hand and British values and culture on the other. Which is not surprising given the influence of the Hebrew Bible and of Judaism on Christianity, particularly on its non-contemplative or pietistic strands.

In the second half of the 19th century, one of the great institutions of British Jewry was founded - the United Synagogue. It was the creation of middle-class Ashkenazi Jews who had come to Britain to join their Sephardi co-religionists. Many were troubled by the foreignness and the religious customs and fervour of the Eastern European immigrants. The United Synagogue embarked upon a conscious policy of Anglicisation. The establishment pursued moderate, conservative policies with a strong dimension of accommodation. Thus religious leaders were referred to as clergy and many even adopted dog-collars. As British Jews established themselves in the suburbs – Maida Vale, St John's Wood,– not a *kippah,* not a skullcap would be seen on the streets. The disagreements with the smaller Federation of Synagogues, which was sympathetic to the practices and customs of the Eastern European immigrants, continue to this day.

What I am trying to illustrate is that Jewish immigration to Britain is characterised by:
(1) a desire to integrate into society, play an active part, enjoy the fruits of belonging and
(2) an equally strong desire not to lose distinctive identity.[11]

---

[11]   This is, of course, to talk in generalities and to express what one might infer to be 'communal policy'. There have been many individual Jews who have sought assimilation for a range of reasons and increasing numbers who have simply been absorbed by an increasingly secular society. I have a hunch that if every Brit with memories of a Jewish ancestor were to return to Judaism, it would not just be the Catholic Church that is out-performing the Church of England!

(3) a preparedness to accommodate and play by the rules;

(4) a drive to succeed – educationally, socially, economically and politically – rooted in the values and psyche of Jews themselves and undoubtedly fostered by the importance that Judaism gives to education;

(5) a coincidence of values, not the least of them those of social justice and social concern, which is hardly surprising given the place of the Hebrew Bible, adopted as the Old Testament, in British culture.

The *Shoah* and the establishment of the State of Israel.

Jews came to Britain both because of persecution and for economic reasons. British foreign policy did not affect Britain's Jews in the same way as foreign policy now affects minority groups. The fact is that most Jewish immigrants to Britain from Eastern Europe between 1881 and 1905 never again saw the families they had left behind.

The middle of the 20th century sees a dramatic change.

First because of the *Shoah*. Of course, the events in Europe impacted upon Jews in Britain – one only has to read the newspapers of the 1930s to see the rising tide of anti-Semitism in Britain. Indeed, there are editorials which are not only offensive to Jews but are so paradigmatic that you only have to change the name of the group to fit later waves of immigration.[12] German and Austrian Jewish refugees made an enormous contribution to British Jewish life as well as to British culture.[13]

All of this pales into relative insignificance beside the effect that the *Shoah* had and continues to have on the psyche of the British Jewish community. I want to stress that you cannot cope with British – indeed European – Jewry unless you are prepared to face the frustration of dealing with people who, more than sixty years on, are still traumatised. You have to be prepared to deal

---

[12] Sunday Express 19th June 1938 is a peach.
[13] The sprinkling of German surnames amongst British Nobel Laureates in Science is a clue.

with the difficult and unpalatable fact that even **British** Jewry is a survivor community, a community of those seeking to make sense of their continuing existence and of the fear and guilt that goes with being survivors.

But that, of course, is not all. Three years after a remnant of Jewry emerged from the mind-numbing obscenity of the *Shoah* (some of whom *tried* to make their way to Palestine, then under British mandate), Jews who had lived for 1900 years as a stateless people without a homeland found they had one at last.

From this point, 1948, the external (i.e. events in Israel) has a profound effect on the internal (i.e. British Jewry, its concerns and self-perception). The image of the British Jew – and his or her self-image – began to change in response to the image of the Israeli, particularly after the Six Day War (40th Anniversary this year). Jews could at last think of themselves as normal, physically strong, successful in worldly terms. It marks the beginning of the wearing of the *kippah* in public on British streets and in British public places. A measure of public distinctiveness begins to replace the deferential and timid accommodation of the Jewish clergyman in a dog collar of the 1930s.[14]

However, the (self-)image of the British Jew as normal, physically strong and successful begins to change almost before there is a chance to enjoy it. The Jew as a reflection of the confident, heroic Israeli quickly turns into the bully and persecutor, the scourge of the underdog – as words like Nazi, Holocaust and Apartheid are flung at Israel in relation to the Palestinians. As the situation in the Middle East becomes more and more intractable and alarming, the realisation begins to dawn upon

---

[14] Clothing is a key indicator of the distinctiveness/separateness spectrum. Note my deliberate blurring of the image of the Israeli and the self-image of the Jew.

Jews that they may be seen both as powerful and ruthless[15] and also as a profound nuisance and even as expendable.[16]

Whilst it is self-evident that not all anti-Zionism and criticism of Israel is anti-Semitic, the statistics bear out an inexorable increase in anti-Semitism in Britain. It's proliferation within the Muslim world[17] and re-importation into Britain are terrifying realities for the Jewish community. The Jewish community is the only significant minority in Britain to have been forced over the last thirty years to maintain high levels of security at all public buildings. Every synagogue and every Sunday school, using volunteers from within the community, has to maintain vigilance at services and at educational, social and cultural events.[18] The cost to the Jewish community – economically and psychologically – is enormous.

The *Shoah* and the establishment of the State of Israel represent events far beyond these shores which have had and continue to have the profoundest possible impact on the Jewish community here. It should be added that in both historical episodes, Britain and British foreign policy have been deeply involved.[19]

The rise of fundamentalism and the conflict with Islam

---

[15] Israel's rapid transformation from David to Goliath is a remarkable feature of the last forty years.
[16] In a world fearful of the arrival of China as a super power and desperate for oil, at which point does Israel get ditched?
[17] Anti-Semitism in the Middle East is a product of 19th century Christian minority communities. It was fanned by Hitler but its huge proliferation and governmental exploitation is essentially of the last fifteen years.
[18] Jews are often outraged that others do not realise this or query the need for it. The need is, of course, confirmed by the police and the security services. The danger comes not from the indigenous far right but from those bound up with events in the Middle East.
[19] This is not meant to be accusatory but simply to observe that British foreign policy – towards Hitler, the Mandate, Palestine, Israel, Iraq – impacts in a variety of ways on the British Jewish community.

A very significant global phenomenon has been the rise of fundamentalism since the 1960s. There is no space here to elaborate.[20] Suffice to say that it is now widely accepted that Judaism, Christianity, Islam, Hinduism and Sikhism have all been affected by a rising tide of fundamentalism throughout the world. Although the term has its origins in the first decade of the 20th century in the United States, the phenomenon is essentially one of the second half of the 20th century. It involves a fearful rejection of the modern world;[21] an attempted recreation of a past existence that never was;[22] a reaffirmation of absolute truths brought into question by modernity;[23] and a willingness to impose those truths on others, by force, by seizing the power of the state if necessary.[24] We are aware of its impact on Islam but it has also impacted on Christianity, particularly in the United States, and Judaism both in Britain and in Israel.

The unexpected resurgence of ultra-Orthodox Judaism in recent decades is undoubtedly part of the phenomenon. Britain's Haredi community, of course, do not manifest the objectionable, violent dimension of fundamentalism. But they do represent an exception to the otherwise consistent British Jewish pattern of actively seeking integration.

There is little need, I think, to elaborate further on the impact of global fundamentalism on the Jewish community in Britain. It has become painfully and inextricably interwoven with Israel in the context of the Middle East conflict. It is worryingly present in Britain itself.

---

[20] See, for instance, the issue of the journal Concilium devoted exclusively to Fundamentalism: Fundamentalism as an Ecumenical Challenge, eds Hans Küng and Jürgen Moltmann, SCM, London, 1992 and particularly the work of M E Marty.
[21] And is therefore 'anti-Western'.
[22] Cf the Taliban fantasy of recreating early Islam.
[23] In an age that has, thankfully, finally dethroned absolutism.
[24] The resurgence of theocracies and competitive proselytisation.

This leads finally to acknowledging the profound significance of the conflict between the Islamic world and the post-Christian West led by America. Jews often feel – not without good reason – that they, in their almost universal identity as Zionists and supporters of Israel, are now seen as the core problem of the world. It is all too often suggested that the world's problems cannot be solved unless the Israel-Palestine conflict is solved. And that solving the Israel-Palestine conflict will bring peace to the globe. This fantasy carries for Jews echoes of long-standing libels and stereotypes. One might add that it is very uncomfortable being a tiny morsel of schnitzel in a very large bread and pitta sandwich. Why did nearly 50% of World Jewry have to end up at precisely the point where the tectonic plates of the post-Christian Western and Islamic worlds meet?

The 'Salad Bowl' model for living within society – integration without assimilation

The majority of British Jews– have espoused the 'integration without assimilation' model for 350 years. Let me suggest a metaphor – that of the salad bowl. What Jews have opted for is society as a salad bowl in which the various 'vegetables' live together within a single bowl, retaining their individual colour, texture and taste whilst contributing to the dish as a whole. Like all metaphors, it is imperfect but it does have certain merits.

First, it rejects the melting pot approach or, to continue the metaphor, the bowl of soup of indeterminate taste and colour. Though it is important to acknowledge that it should not prevent the individual from opting to merge into wider, secular society if she or he so chooses. This has actually proved the greatest threat to the Jewish diaspora 'experiment' but it is the right of each individual.

Second, it raises the issue of 'parallel lives'. This was a phrase which first appeared in a report on riots in a handful of northern towns – where immigrant communities were living parallel lives.[25] In other words, they were isolated vegetables, untouched by the other vegetables in the salad bowl, neither contributing to the whole nor being much affected by it. My own view is that this is not a very desirable model. There are small Jewish communities which adopt a relatively isolated stance – both out of fidelity to the primacy of their culture and as a survival strategy. I concede that in a democratic society it has to be the right of groups not to join the salad bowl, not to integrate to any meaningful extent. But I wonder how much it should be encouraged by government and given financial support?

The issue is particularly complex because all the significant examples that I can think of in this country are of groups whose broader attachments lie not in this country but abroad.[26] An understanding of multiple identities has helped us move beyond paralysing debates over dual loyalties. But there is an important discussion – albeit a dangerous one – that must be had over the extent to which the 'neither integrate nor assimilate' strategy is one that should be actively supported by Government. Does society have the right to encourage the integrationist strategy whilst being either neutral or discouraging towards the deliberate adoption of 'parallel lives' or self imposed isolation? It must be true that whilst immigrant groups with strong attachments to others abroad will always be affected by British foreign policy, the greater the integration, the greater the stake in British society, the easier it is to manage conflicts of interests and allegiance.

The success of immigration

I have suggested that the Jewish immigration into this country has succeeded because Jews have played by the rules; been moderate and unthreatening as they have sought change (for instance in the 19th century to their legal and constitutional

---

[25] The riots took place in Bradford, Burnley and Oldham in the summer of 2001.
[26] Unlike, for instance, the Amish in the USA.

rights); have got on and contributed to British society; and have used a consonance of values to good effect.

It is not often asked whether the Jewish immigration into Britain has been a success from a Jewish point of view. It has, but with one major reservation. Jewish numbers have never been large. The community peaked at 390,000 in 1950 and is declining steadily. The Jewish population of Britain according to the 2001 census is 267,000.

That raises a crucial question. Is it in fact possible for a minority group to integrate into British society and yet retain its distinctiveness and avoid assimilation? We should acknowledge that the decline in Jewish numbers in Britain is caused by Jews leaving the community in favour of secular society, *aliyah*,[27] a low birth rate – all of them voluntary factors, matters of individual choice. But that doesn't detract from the question and therefore the viability of the model from the point of view of the minority community. Is the salad bowl sustainable? And if it isn't, what are the implications for the kind of society we wish to create and some immigrant groups think they are joining?

The Jewish community has fallen from 1st place to 4th place over a period of 50 years in terms of size of non-Christian religious minority groups in Britain. During those 50 years it has become remarkably proficient at working with government and engaging with government in order to protect Jewish interests. Its networking ability is very impressive. But the fact is that, compared, say, to the Muslim community the Jewish community is now relatively unimportant when it comes to national and international political judgements. We have seen in France how Jewish interests have been sacrificed because dealing with the Muslim community is so much more important. We have seen in France how the accommodation or the contract – you can wear **small** distinguishing items such as a skullcap or a Star of David in school, a contract developed over many years – has been discarded in favour of no articles of religious identification at all –

---

[27] Literally 'going up' i.e. going to live in Israel.

because the French state and the Muslim community could not come to the same accommodation.[28] Jews in this country are genuinely afraid of being sacrificed on the altar of expediency or national interest. And of disappearing off the radar – off religious education syllabuses and off foreign policy judgements.

Numbers should never be underestimated as a factor in minority psychology and reality. They affect self-perception, group agenda and status. They have important implications for national policy.

Insecurity: a function of primarily external factors

Living with insecurity is second nature to Jews. For the last thousand years Jews have frequently lived a precarious existence within Christian communities and held the status of second class citizens in Muslim societies.[29] Why are there no Jewish equivalents of the great cathedrals? The answer is not just a function of numbers and wealth but of a lack of sense of permanence and security in making such physical statements. Why have Jews been prominent in the diamond trade? Because diamonds are amongst the most portable forms of wealth and therefore well suited to people who never know when they will have to move on.

However, as we have seen, two episodes within 20th century history have profoundly affected the psyche even of Jews inured to insecurity. The first is the *Shoah*.

Its effect has been that European Jewry has tended to see itself and still tends to see itself primarily as victim. It is both

---

[28] This is not intended as a value judgement on Muslim policies over women's dress.

[29] Jews, by and large, have fared better under Islam than under Christianity. The considerable exodus from Christian Europe into the Ottoman Empire is illustrative. But the contrast can be overstated. See Jews, Turks, Ottomans: A Shared History, Fifteen Through the Twentieth Century, ed Avigdor Levy, Syracuse UP, 2002.

understandable and truthful. But I would like to quote an American Jewish scholar, Diana Pinto. Sixty years on and with the challenge of an expanding Europe here and now, she asserts:

> "1. Jews should stop thinking of themselves as the victims of the Holocaust and of anti-Semitism, and consider themselves as the full-fledged, integrated and positive actors they are across Europe.
> 2. The time has come to restore the image of the humanist Jew fighting for universal causes beyond his group's own interests extended at most to targeted 'coalitions'.
> 3. Jewish history must be presented for it own inherently positive content and not as a subset of an anti-Semitic saga, with the negative defining the positive.
> 4. The Holocaust must be reintegrated into its own historic time, to restore the political context in which it took place, so that it no longer stands as a sacrosanct black light, cutting Jews off from the rest of humanity.
> 5. Jews, on the basis of their iconic value, are in the best position for the rewriting of a *res publica* contract, which can balance identity needs with shared universal principles in the creation of an open, tolerant but value-laden space."[30]

One might sum Pinto up by saying that the Jewish experience – and Europe's experience of Jews – can be extraordinarily helpful in constructing the kind of society – of multiple identities, of shared universal principles, of open, tolerant but value laden space, of coalitions of diversity held by common citizenship – that paves the way for a cohesive, pluralistic future. But the sense of victimhood – *today present not just in Jews* – makes it doubly difficult.

It is seldom acknowledged that more than 80% of world Jewry lives either in Israel or in the United States. Within a generation

---

[30] Diana Pinto, Are There Jewish Answers to Europe's Questions? European Judaism, pp 55-7, 06/2, vol 39 no2.

50% of world Jewry will live in Israel. Those two statistics mean that Israel is irrevocably and indissolubly tied to American foreign policy whether that policy be wise or misguided. That isn't the best place for Israel to be long term but it is hard to see how Israel could be anywhere else. Furthermore, most Jews believe that the destruction of Israel would finally bring about the end of Jews and Judaism. That fear is one of the dominating forces in Jewish life.

The impact of global events and foreign policy

It is really illuminating to reflect that sixty years ago, a Jewish community of 390,000 (even that, a figure swollen by refugees who were not to stay here) represented the largest non-Christian minority in Britain.

The composition of British society has changed remarkably in the last sixty years and is continuing to do so. The Times recently reported[31] that the Catholic Church has now overtaken the Church of England for the first time since the Reformation because of the impact of migration from Catholic countries in the last few years.

This change has happened at precisely the same time as a globalisation of communications has taken place – Christians, Jews, Muslims, Hindus and Sikhs know what is happening to their fellow Christians in the Sudan, their fellow Jews in Israel, their fellow Muslims in Iraq and their fellow Hindus and Sikhs in India *as it is actually happening.*

We are now witnessing the globalisation of struggles – between the West and Islam, between rich and poor, between developed and developing – and those struggles, by virtue of the globalisation of communications and the globalisation of populations, touch us here in Britain at every point.

---

[31] The Times, 15th February 2007

I want to say a final word about the globalisation of fundamentalism. Fundamentalism is a profound reaction against the modern or post-modern world. It is fearful, reactionary and reasserts values of absolutism, proselytisation and imperialism which are antithetical to the values which liberal religion and liberal secularism espouse. By and large the great faiths have failed the challenge presented by fundamentalism – failing to tackle fundamentalist tendencies within their respective traditions, failing to combat the attraction of the spurious certainties advanced, failing to address their own failings which help give fundamentalism its attraction and power.

The continuing power of the doctrine of creationism in the United States amongst Christians; the disproportionate power exerted by the settlers and their Knesset allies in Israel; and the extraordinary ability of Islamists or Islamic fundamentalists to justify obscene behaviour to their own populations – all these are a testimony to the power of fundamentalism.

Along with religious fundamentalism we have seen the rise of secular fundamentalism – manifested in the repulsive brutality of sections of the Animal Rights Movement and the mindless insistence in some quarters of publishing cartoons offensive to Islam knowing that they would cause distress to millions of people as a bloody-minded assertion of the principle of free speech. In very many ways, religious fundamentalism and secular fundamentalism have more in common with each other than either do with religious liberalism and secular liberalism.

Which brings me to a final point which may well not belong under this heading but needs to be noted somewhere. The recent debate over gay adoptions troubled me. As a Jewish religious liberal, I am utterly committed to the rights of gays and lesbians and was delighted to support Norwood, the Jewish community's adoption agency, in standing its ground and offering adoption services to Jewish gays and lesbians. But the argument, the conflict, did raise in my mind a very serious question.

I am happy to live in a secular society or, rather, a society with a secular framework. History has discredited theocracies. But what space exists within a modern Western secular society like Britain for religious dissent? Is there no room for any departure from secular principles? We have been asserting the dignity of difference between the faiths and arguing for a plurality of ideals and paths. But what of the dignity of difference between the secular and the religious? The American Jewish philosopher Eugene Borowitz speaks of Jews as commanded to live in "creative maladjustment" with society. One immediately thinks of Abraham Joshua Heschel marching side by side with Martin Luther King. Today religion appears to have handed over its prophetic and power-challenging role to liberal secularism. At the very least, it needs *some* space to recover and express its fundamental but non-fundamentalist purpose.

What may be paradigmatic in the Jewish experience?

It is clear that the Jewish community – from its return in 1656, through the establishment of its early institutions such as the Board of Deputies; through its response to the Eastern European immigration of 1881-1905; and throughout the 20th century – has maintained a contract with government and society. It was and is an unwritten contract but then this is a country with an unwritten constitution.

What I would like to do is to refer back through this paper and try to identify how the terms of a contract, a *res publica* contract to echo Pinto, between an immigrant/minority group and government might look today.

Before I do so, let me recount two episodes from the last few months.

The first is Jack Straw's famous encounter in Blackburn with the veiled Muslim woman. He asked her to remove her veil so that he could have a conversation with her. The episode is clearly about meeting face to face and about the barriers to a real encounter between two human beings. It is doubly symbolic since the veil was not just a barrier to meeting face to face but was read by Straw as a statement of intention not to integrate, not to engage but to remain insulated from the wider community in this country. That may or may not have been a correct reading of the woman's intentions but it raises the issue of whether minority groups have the right to remain separate, to live 'parallel' lives. Should government actively discourage veiled or separate living and if so by what means?

The second is politically difficult for me personally to raise but I will do so because it is important. There are a number of ultra-Orthodox Jewish groups of various kinds, collectively referred to as the *Haredi* community. Because their tradition is for the men to engage in study as much as possible and therefore not always to work and because they do not use modern methods of birth control and have large families, these groups experience real poverty. They have built up a network of private schools providing schooling tailored to their needs. Current Board of Deputies policy is to encourage these schools to join the State system and to encourage government to fund them. It is clear that government funding for the schools is a way of addressing poverty. It is less clear whether this is an effective strategy to encourage a greater degree of integration and involvement with wider society. Supposing State funding were to alleviate (self-imposed) hardship but did not clearly promote integration, would it be an appropriate use of public funds?

I believe that the two 'cases' referred to above go to the heart of the contract that needs to be clarified and developed.

Here are some suggested terms.

Immigrant/Faith Group Contract with Government and Society

The Group should demonstrate:
- Commitment to the fundamental values of modern British society – social justice, democracy, equality, tolerance, respect for the individual, pluralism.

- Commitment to working actively with others to build a just and cohesive society.
- Commitment to share its values for the good of humanity and the globe.[32]
- Commitment to civic and political involvement.
- Commitment to reflect on its own psyche and narrative and to understand the psyche and narratives of others and the interaction between the two. This involves a commitment to self-criticism.
- Commitment to a multi-faith society in which faith is expressed in such a way as to allow space for other faiths and in which faiths recognise that they can only exist in relation to each other.
- Commitment to the adage: 'take care of your own soul and another person's body not your own body and another person's soul'[33]
- Commitment to recognising that a minority group is 'only' a minority group and that the majority has rights too, particularly in respect of the longstanding culture and traditions of the country.
- Commitment to recognising that government foreign policy, if conducted on the basis of the interests of society at large and on the basis of the best values of our society, may conflict with minority group loyalties and aspects of identity. Commitment of its leaders to working with government to minimise the distress this may cause to members of the minority community.

I would not impose these terms on asylum seekers. Those fleeing for their lives have a special call and our laws should provide us with sufficient protection. But in an age of mass

---

[32] The allusion here is to the crucial work of the Catholic theologian Hans Küng, particularly in Global Responsibility, SCM, London, 1991. "There can be no peace in the world without peace between the religions". The peace must be based upon a self-critical assessment of what each faith can best contribute to the good of humanity and the globe.

[33] Hasidic.

migration and I can see no reason to object to a contract in circumstances other than asylum seeking.

Government and Society

- Commitment to allowing the group the space and resources to maintain itself.
- Commitment to understanding and respect for the particularity of minority communities including the needs of members of a group to live in proximity to other members of that group.
- Commitment to allowing and encouraging the group to push back the envelope of rights where there is not yet full equality.
- Whilst basing our approach to immigration significantly on economic and social factors, commitment to recognising the concern of immigrant groups for other members of that group who are suffering economic as well as social and political hardship.
- Commitment to making every effort to understand the psyche and narrative of minority groups and responding appropriately.
- Commitment to protecting minority groups against hatred and resentment. Accepting that the security of minority groups is not just a responsibility for the group but is also a wider, societal responsibility.
- Commitment to providing quality education and facilitating social, cultural and economic integration.
- Commitment to giving positive support to the survival of immigrant groups, their cultural heritage and what they can give to enrich society.
- Commitment to respecting the desire not to assimilate.
- Commitment to being sensitive to multiple identities and allegiances which may conflict with British foreign policy and the national interest.
- Commitment to understanding how foreign policy and events abroad impact on groups within Britain; commitment to anticipating any likely negative effects

and adopting positive strategies for minimising tension and conflict
- Commitment to recognising the rights of religious groups to dissent from accepted secular norms and recognising that there are times when imposing secular norms will cause more pain and distress than is gained by the imposition.

Rabbi Dr Tony Bayfield is Head of The Movement for Reform Judaism and Lecturer in Personal Theology, Leo Baeck College, London. The Reform Movement is the second largest organisation of synagogues in Britain.

A Clash of Civilisations – the Paradox of Globalisation?

Sadiq Khan MP

At the end of the Cold war international political theorists and politicians alike, sought to find explanations of a world in which the conceptual simplicity of three distinct, ideologically divergent, blocs no longer applied[34]. Initially, the most influential vision of how the post Cold War world would unfold saw a single force, globalisation, as laying the foundations for global peace and prosperity by narrowing the difference of values between cultures, spreading democracy, and uniting all nations in a single global economy.

The terrorist atrocities on September 11th 2001 (9/11) shattered this illusion. Far from ushering in a period of international harmony, globalisation seemed to some to be provoking a backlash and setting up a conflict between the West and the Rest, giving credence to the argument that we will soon experience what Samuel P Huntington coined the 'clash of civilisations'[35].

This metaphor has clearly taken hold of popular imagination and thus been easily reinforced by the way that contemporary events have panned out. 9/11, the subsequent 'War on Terror', the July 7th bombings in London in 2005 and the recent fracas over cartoons depicting the Prophet Mohammed have all been tacitly accepted as confirmation that our values are unique to our culture and not compatible with others.

The argument to be presented in this chapter questions the inevitability of this situation. It is my view that globalisation both

---

[34] This refers to the division of the planet during the Cold War where the First World represented the West, the Second World the Soviet Bloc and the Third World the non-alaigned countries.
[35] Samuel P. Huntington, The Clash of Civilizations, *Foreign Affairs*, Vol. 22, Summer 1993

homogenises *and* fragments cultures within and between 'civilisations', which does not lead to violent conflict or religious extremism. I hope to demonstrate this point; firstly by raising concerns with the terms of the current debate and the application of the lexicon 'civilisation' and secondly by showing that these two forces of globalisation do operate in a mutually dependent relationship, aiding and abetting each other. Finally, I will touch upon how and why we should move away form the divisive rhetoric of civilisations.

Cultures, not 'civilisations'

'Civilisation' is thought to be culture *writ large*; the broadest form of identity one can associate with. A civilisation therefore expresses all those things a society has in common, for example its historical, linguistic and religious elements. These cultural factors in turn determine the nature and character of each civilisation. They are by definition unique and it is this uniqueness that seems under threat from globalisation.

In practice, 'culture' and 'civilisation' are often used interchangeably, but there is an important difference. There may be specific cultural features that hold true across what is broadly defined as a civilisation, but we lose the ability to detect them if our analysis focuses only on the broader entity. Religious and cultural groups such as Islam and the West can be meaningfully discussed, but only if it is acknowledged that they are more complex and diverse than these labels account for.

With this in mind, it is possible to analyse whether civilisational (cultural) differentiation is increasing in today's world, which runs contrary to the expected impact of globalisation on cultural assimilation.

Globalisation of culture

Economics has arguably become the dominant discourse in debates about globalisation. The interconnectedness and interdependency of the global economy is indisputable. But, even though international trade and finance are undoubtedly important, economic globalisation is just one dimension of a phenomenon that also has political and cultural, including religious, elements[36].

Benjamin Barber antagonistically frames the analysis of cultural globalisation, and the issues surrounding cultural assimilation, as "Jihad vs. McWorld", which has now taken on some resonance as a battle between Islam and The West[37]. These concepts represent the two sides of globalisation, which operate simultaneously. McWorld represents the homogenising materialism of consumer culture, which is emblemised by the instantly recognisable logos McDonald's, Coca-Cola and MTV. McWorld is tied together by communications, information, entertainment and commerce that enforce integration and uniformity. The trend of McWorld to promote a materialistic culture (that embodies, not the higher ideals of the West and modernity – such as human rights and democracy – but its baser aspects of greed and consumerism), has provoked the reassertion of local identities[38] that Barber has dubbed 'Jihad'. This analysis anticipates the retribalisation of peoples and a return to traditional religious, rather than global, identities, as a response to the threat of McWorld, which is often regarded as "American imperialism" and an instrument of soft power, rather than a benign extra-national force.

Although pitted against each other and striving for opposite ends, Jihad and McWorld are themselves, paradoxically, mutually dependant; for example, it is only through mass media and new innovations in communications technology that Jihad is able to impact upon the McWorld[39]. There are plenty of examples of this curious relationship, but perhaps none demonstrate the paradox at its core more clearly as the instance of fundamentalist

---

[36] Tomlinson, J. *'Globalisation and Culture'* (1999) p. 17
[37] Benjamin Barber, *Jihad vs. McWorld: How Globalism And Tribalism Are Reshaping The World* (1996)
[38] Sadowski, Y. *'The Myth of Global Chaos'* (1998) p. 39
[39] *Ibid* p. 5

conspiracies being plotted on the World Wide Web, where global culture can give local culture its medium and audience[40].

Despite the explicit attempt to equate 'Jihad vs. McWorld' with 'Islam vs. the West', the competition between them does not only take place within that empirical setting. Resistance to the homogenising effects of McWorld is not restricted to civilisational and religious distinctions, and does not only take place in societies outside the West. The dynamics of the Jihad-McWorld relationship are evident in Western Europe, the Far-East and *within* Islamic countries, to varying degrees. The French government, for example, attacks 'franglais' whilst at the same time funding 'EuroDisney', McDonald's remains the most popular eatery in Japan, despite a re-emergence of its cultural traditions[41], and, in China, in spite of the apparent rise of Chinese nationalism, the first scientific poll revealed that a commitment to materialism had eclipsed traditional Confucian or Communist values – 68 percent of people when asked about their 'personal philosophy' responded "work hard and get rich"[42]. These examples highlight the fact that globalisation creates commonalities between what are thought of as the most distinct cultures, whilst provoking a backlash from all that it penetrates. There are no examples of any civilisation acting as one united, monolithic system and no one group can legitimately claim to speak for an entire civilisation, but they are often treated as such, leading to distorted generalisations and sometimes conflict.

Avoiding the Clash

The propensity to treat different elements of a culture or society as a unified entity is particularly prevalent when the 'Islamic civilisation' is discussed in the mainstream media in the West. Islam, the Arabs and the Muslim world are represented as a monolithic bloc, poised against the West. This is especially so in

---

[40] *Ibid* p. 17
[41] *Ibid* p. 18
[42] Sadowski, Y. *'The Myth of Global Chaos'* (1998) p. 41. Poll published in *'Wall Street Journal'* on May 2nd 1995

the area of freedom of speech. This was illustrated by the recent cartoon crisis which has been depicted by some in the West as a clash of civilizations *par excellance*: a fundamental conflict of values between absolute religious beliefs on the one hand and absolute political principles on the other; between God's word (as interpreted by man) and the freedoms said to be enshrined in 'Enlightened' Western liberal democracy. Not only, however, is such a view mistaken (the cartoons crisis cannot be considered a clash of civilisations in the strict sense that Huntington would accept, occurring as it did in mainland Europe and with neither civilisation speaking with one 'voice'), it also misses the point. Where the clash, or at least the clash in this instance, seemed to rear its ugly head was with regards to how the West and the Rest (here Islam) deal with the problem of cultural integration – and, in particular, the level of accommodation (or even tact and good taste) which should be afforded journalistically to particular minority groups. For instance, in many respects some people in the West were complicit in contributing to the notion of a clash of civilisations with regard to the cartoons, not simply for printing pictures of Mohammed with his turban pierced with a bomb (a depiction if not certain to cause dissent almost certain to cause misunderstanding), but rather because many thought that not doing so would be to acquiesce to religious tyranny and thereby threaten the existence of Western secular identity. Indeed, whilst religious fundamentalism - that is, the Islamic rule that forbids the making of images of its highest Prophet – may have appeared to force the issue, political fundamentalism – that is, the insistence on freedom of speech regardless of offence – inflamed it[43].

However, such occurrences are lauded as archetypal examples of the incompatibility of religious and secular culture and implicitly the incompatibility of Islam in the West, despite the fact that, as so often is the case, the violent protests came only from a very small minority of people claiming to represent a much larger group. Furthermore, within predominantly Muslim countries, secular identities are beginning to assert themselves. A recent

---

[43] Philip Kennicott, Clash Over Cartoons is a Caricature of Civilization, Washington Post, 4 February 2006

example is the hundreds of thousands of Turkish citizens who marched on Istanbul in support of secularism in Turkey and to denounce the connection between the President and political Islam. Members of the European Union (EU) should recognise actions of this sort and acknowledge the changes being made in Turkey. Large steps towards meeting the criteria for EU membership have been made, including improvements in Turkey's human rights record. Failure to acknowledge this progress perpetuates the common feeling in countries outside the EU that it is a "Christian Club", with a distinct civilisation, which does not open its doors the countries with a different majority religion and culture, due to a perceived clash of civilisations.

The example of the cartoon crisis and the debate surrounding Turkey's entry to the EU highlights a broader problem created by associating disparate groups and presuming that any one fraction can speak for them all. It is not only the media that are culprits in exacerbating this situation. Since 9/11 'The West' has been embroiled in a 'war on terror' declared on our behalf by the American administration. A war against an abstract concept is, by definition, unwinnable, but more crucially, referring to different terrorist cells as a single tangible entity with enough cohesion to be a viable enemy, gives them an authority and credibility that they do not deserve[44]. This point has now finally been recognised by the Government and the phrase is no longer in official use[45].

Changing the rhetoric of the current political debate on foreign policy is an important step in tempering relations and perception between British Muslims and the wider community. The vocal minority skewer the general perception of the majority of British Muslims who can incorporate the principles of free speech and

---

[44] Sadiq Khan MP and Leni Wild *Rethinking UK security policy* IN *Politics for a New Generation* ippr (2007)

[45] In April 2007 Secretary of State for International Development, Hilary Benn MP, gave a speech to the New York based think-tank Centre on International Cooperation explaining that British Ministers and civil servants no longer use the phrase.

other liberal values into their religious practice. Renouncing the idea that we can have a "war on terror" implicitly directed at the Islamic faith goes some way to dispel the misconception formed by grouping people together in broad-brush strokes. But more needs to be done to ensure that the common stereotype of unassimilated, isolationist Muslims is dismissed and to ensure that that this stereotype is not prophetically self fulfilling amongst minority Muslim groups in Western countries and amongst Muslims in Britain in particular.

One way of meeting this challenge is by engaging British Muslims in the formal political process. This is particularly important in regards to foreign policy making, which is currently used as a campaigning tool by extremists, but also relevant to other mainstream policy areas where minority communities' views appear underrepresented. Substantive representation of minority communities is one way of restoring faith in the policy making process and allaying concerns that it deliberately targets Muslims both in this country and abroad. Recent events have obscured some of the ostensibly humanitarian efforts made by the Labour Government toward Muslim countries, including interventions in Kosovo and extensive aid and educational programmes in South Asia and Africa. However, the responsibility for meeting the challenge must not just rest with the UK (and the West). It is essential for Muslim majority countries to better understand and relate to the cultural norms, rationale and principles behind some of the UK Government's actions. In this regard the 'soft power' of UK citizens with family members, friends and business contacts overseas is crucial. There are plenty of integrated British Muslims that prove supporters of Huntington's thesis wrong and there is an onus on them, as well as all people who share their values, to demonstrate the compatibility of different cultures.

Conclusion

A clash of civilisations becomes relevant domestically when you are living in a multicultural and multi religious society like the UK. The fact that the four men responsible for the terrorist actions on

7th July 2005 were born and raised in Britain and claimed to be Muslims has been extolled by supporters of Huntington's thesis as an example of what happens when the two forces of globalisation meet and people try to associate with more than one identity. However, this simplistic notion fails to take into account the fact that the vast majority of British Muslims not only abhorred and condemned the actions unequivocally, but do manage to practice their faith whilst maintaining a British identity. Moreover, the concept of 'multiple identities' is not unique to British Muslims. It is commonplace to form some attachment of identity beyond your immediate society, whether it is a feeling of religious solidarity or a commitment to a particular set of values. Recognising this fact is important if we are going to be successful in restoring trust in our foreign policy and using, to all of our advantage, the experience and informed views of people who have a particular vested interest in bringing peace to the Middle East, which at the moment seems like the biggest foreign policy challenge we face.

Sadiq Khan MP is the Member of Parliament for Tooting. He is the Parliamentary Private Secretary to the Rt Hon Jack Straw MP, Leader of the House of Commons and a member of the Public Accounts Select Committee.[46]

---

[46] Many thanks to Leah Kreitzman for her useful background research for this chapter.

Religion and British Foreign Policy

Gautam Banerji

Religion is an ancient part of human legacy and a pervasive part of human history. However, religion in the present day context came to the scene in a sense not by the strength of an argument but by the power of events. The horrific images of suicide bombs and subway attacks make us all aware that the power of religious politics in the twenty first century cannot be ignored, or rather should not be ignored. At the same time the possibilities of religious politics are richer and more enduring than the momentary flashes of the extremist bombs would lead us to believe. There is a need today, than ever before, to infuse a truly religious dimension into the political order throughout the world. A systematic attention to religion therefore is at least important to set the facts right.

Hinduism demands that no man do to another what would be repugnant to himself. This is not at odds with the tenets of every other major religion, Islam not excepted. Hindu formulations of religious politics attempts to hold the world order together in a bond of kinship founded upon principles of mutuality and interdependence. The old maxim *Vasudhaiva kutumbakam* (the world is one extended family) unfolds a new meaning in a world torn asunder today by endless, selfish strife where globalism has come to mean free and unhindered access to the world's wealth and resources for the rich and on their own terms.

Free trade is held out as a panacea to alleviate world poverty. The global marketplace, however, remains far from level, where the poor compete on unequal terms with the rich. While it is recognised that world poverty remains a threat to peace and sustainable development, the rich continue to do business by their rules and standards, and prosper. The poor continue to be poorer. There is a need to rectify this imbalance expeditiously in the interest of lasting peace in the world. The onus lies on global players to take the lead in this effort.

By virtue of our geography, our history and our people, Britain is certainly a global player. To a considerable extent our foreign policy is motivated by our efforts to preserve our global interests. However, it is wrong to assume that British foreign policy today is a motivating factor in radicalising young Muslims in the country. Tony Blair has constantly denied that his foreign policy and military operations could be blamed for driving Muslim youths into the arms of terror. And he is not wrong. That British foreign policy was oppressing Muslims, is, in the words of Blair, "rubbish" to say the least. The claim that British foreign policy was driving Muslim youths into the clutches of terrorists was put forward by no other than Mohammed Siddique Khan, one of the July 7 suicide bombers. To submit to such reasoning would amount to playing into the hands of terror.

What remains enigmatic, however, is the stark reality that Islamic fundamentalism remains entrenched in the midst of the material prosperity of present-day Britain. If the fault line has to be drawn, it is to be found in the failure of the system to allow large chunks of the population the advantages of social integration. Much to our consternation, Britain remains a highly fragmented society where many struggle to find their rightful place under the sun while some remain too much under it. It has an element of rigidity even less accommodating than the archaic Hindu caste system. Minority communities meet with a glass ceiling in every attempt at social mobility. Diversity remains a convenient political slogan with an inert capacity of the majority to celebrate it in all its ramifications. Such a social milieu breeds social mismatches and misfits.

Just as there is a need to address issues of inequity and inequality at the macro level, there is a need to do so at the micro level as well; and that too on a war footing. This would be the right approach to the war on terror.

We Hindus as a people had lived in peace and amity with Muslims through centuries in the Indian sub-continent. Inspired by our saints and seers, Sufism struck a harmonious chord with the native faith of the sub-continent. This was at a time when medieval Europe was launching crusades against the onslaught of Islam for its survival. While Christianity and Islam clashed and swords rattled, India witnessed a rich synthesis of thoughts and ideas flowing in through trade and intercourse. We were then in a world harmonized through mutual trust and faith. There was a deep spiritual dimension to the inter-dependence that was never compromised.

The world today unfolds a different story. We as a people, who lived with Islam in peace and harmony, witness a religious apartheid imported into Britain by religious fundamentalism with its sinister roots in the same region that saw the flowering of Sufi mysticism with its message of universal harmony. We remain grieved to be told that Baha'is do not find a place for study in Iranian universities. We are equally grieved to read about religious indoctrination in schools of present day Pakistan where Hindus are held out as idolators and heretics. The Hindu Council UK, under the capable leadership of Anil Bhanot, continues its collective efforts to uphold human dignity and counter religious bigots wherever they are confronted. We remain at the same time acutely aware of the inherent danger of some Hindus being driven into religious bigotry, which we will continue to resist.

As a community, we Hindus are an integral part of British society today. We pride ourselves in being British in the first instance, drawing our cultural identity from a legacy of five thousand years with its origins through the sojourns of our ancestors in the green pastures of Central Asia before it took roots through settled life in the Indian sub-continent. Hinduism has so much enriched the life and culture of present day Britain, drawing upon the heritage we have brought to it.

We look forward to a synthesis of our mutual culture and traditions as we move through the pages of history here in Britain in the days to come. We look forward to the day we invite every Briton to celebrate the advent of spring with us with a splash of colour in the festival of Holi. We do also invite all to join in the celebration of the Festival of Lights where we hold out a beacon of hope in the midst of despondency and gloom. We would then re-write our almanac to make this essential spring festival coincide with the advent of daffodils and celebrate Deepavali in the bleak mid-winter of the British Isles. But this needs a new awakening, a new understanding of everything that is India, that is 'Hindu' at its best.

Through the past two centuries, British foreign policy was as much guided by "realpolitik" as other powers in Europe. And at the core of this "realpolitik" was the centrality of Britain's imperial interest in India. The crucial importance of India in shaping British foreign policy in the forty years before the First World War need not be underscored here since it remains well documented through the pages of recent history. At the same time India continues to remain equally relevant to British diplomacy today.

While India begins to emerge as a major power in Asia and the Indian Ocean region, it is compelled to shed many of the post-independence ideas on the conduct of foreign policy and called upon to provide security to other states in its neighbourhood. Some of the old themes of British Indian foreign policy today therefore demand far greater attention by policy makers and the political class as a whole.

In responding effectively to the new diplomatic challenges, an understanding of the foreign policy of British India is no doubt the key. At the same time it has to be matched by a new understanding of the role the diaspora here in Britain has to assume in taking the relationship into the twenty first century with maturity and to the benefit of both nations.

There was a time when men saw the East in all her glory. We have lost that vision and are the poorer. Yet we have lost it because we have grown richer. Our standards have altered.

Our Europe is no longer the little Christendom of Gothic times, living on the scanty produce of grey skies, trembling at every rumour of Saladin or the victorious Turks. The early voyagers to the East came from evil smelling walled towns where folk dwelt in kennels and died like flies of epidemic caused by their own insanitation. To men who lived in the cold and changed their clothes once a year and went unwashed for months, the sunshine and the clean water, the children splashing all day in the creeks, the girls at the well were one long delight.

We as a community, like many others moved to the West in a different period but with similar deprivation suffered through a different context. Britain for many of us provided new hopes, new aspirations as we have lived here with dignity. We have acquired self-confidence in the process. And as taught by our seers, we never hesitated to give back more than we took.

We as a community have a role to play in spiritualising British foreign policy. The key to our success will lie in our capacity to give more than we take. We shall continue that effort.

Gautam Banerji is the Executive Member for Legal and Social Protection of the Hindu Council UK. He is enrolled as a Solicitor of the Supreme Court of England and previously worked for twelve years for UNICEF.

How do we tell the real story?

Anthony Bailey, KCSS,

There is an uncomfortable disjuncture in Britain between the perception of interfaith tension and the reality of interfaith co-operation and friendship. This has much to do with the media. What is newsworthy is exceptional; and thank God, it is still exceptional to find hostility across interfaith boundaries. Just as British people, fed by a newspaper diet of crime stories, are far more likely to believe themselves likely to be robbed or mugged than the statistics show they will be, so they believe that religion is a source of antagonism both in Britain and the world. Young people often cite conflict between faiths as a reason not to subscribe to any particular religion, preferring a vaguely deistic universalism to concrete, incarnated traditions of prayer and theology in the belief that this will further peace.

Long before 11 September 2001 there was an entrenched belief that the Christian West and Islamic world were at odds with each other, a belief shadowed by persistent prejudices in both worlds: against an aggressive, imperialist, Crusader West, and of Islam as a religion of war and violence. The news out of the Middle East – and especially recent terrorist attacks on western and Arab cities - feed those prejudices, hardening them. A clash of religions – the Huntingdon thesis - is far more interesting, because it is alarming, than the quotidian business of co-operation and trust.

Perhaps one of our greatest challenges – one I plan to take seriously in my new post as Chairman of the Labour Party's Faith Task Force – is how to counteract this perception with the humdrum reality of warm relationships between Christians, Muslims and Jews, which are more like the gatherings of relatives (and relatives, of course, can be tempestuously intolerant of each other) than of antagonists. I want to help the Party to address more effectively the concerns of the faith communities, and to communicate even better the Party's concerns to those communities. Many recent episodes point to the need for a better bridge between the two as the Party's decision to create the Task Force recognises.

How do we tell the stories of these relationships, in order to encourage them, and to challenge public perception? It is a task for anyone who cares about the future of faith and peace in the human community. Distortions of reality are deathly, because they create downward spirals of mistrust. The truth sets us free from conflict.

One of the positive consequences of 9/ll has been the greater interest in the history of the relationship between the faiths. Huntingdon may have scared the press with talk of a return to religious fratricide, but historians have challenged him with the evidence that the past is not, after all, a story of *odium theologicum* spilling over into war. A recent book by the Middle East expert Zachary Karabell, *People of the Book: the Forgotten History of Islam and the West* – published in the US as *Peace Be Upon You* - is one of many that have sought to tell the forgotten history of the relations between the three faiths, to "reclaim the legacy of coexistence" which is the truer story. While scholars have not lost sight of this history that awareness has remained locked away in libraries. "As a result," Karabell says, "in America and in Europe all that most people hear is the echo of the Arab conquests that followed Muhammad's death. And in the Muslim world the memory of imperialism and Western aggression obscures memories of co-operation."

But focussing on conflict, he says, is "like skipping every other page while reading a book. It isn't just incomplete; it's misleading to the point of incoherence." The conflicts and eruptions of misunderstanding have been real enough; and modern inter-faith co-operation must always start from a contrite acknowledgement of the blood spilled and the injustices committed. But they need to be set in the wider context of alliances, interaction, and co-operation. Relationships break down, but only because they are relationships, just as marital strife can only happen to married couples.

The forgotten story of Christians, Muslims and Jews living co-operatively with each other over the centuries needs to be rescued, just as the equivalent modern story needs to be told. Judaism was central to the formation of Islam; and for a millennium and a half, Jews under Muslim rule enjoyed more safety, freedom and autonomy than under Christian rule. These were pre-enlightenment, pre-secular societies; non-Muslims (dhimmi citizens) did not have equal status; nor did non-Christians in medieval Europe. But they co-existed, mostly in peace, learning from each other; and great civilisations resulted.

The theological interaction between the three faiths has been a constant throughout the centuries, as a British Library exhibition of Jewish, Christian and Muslim holy books – "Sacred: what we share" – is currently placing on display. One of the two royal patrons of that exhibition, King Mohammed VI of Morocco, has the historic religious title of Commander of the Faithful, a unique role in the Muslim world which comes from his direct descend from the Prophet Mohammed. His late father, King Hassan II, was also the first Arab ruler to invite a Pope (John Paul II) to celebrate an open-air Mass, and Jews and Christians in Morocco have full religious freedoms.

The King of Bahrain and the Emir of Qatar has given land to Jews and Christians to build synagogues and churches in their countries. Qatar hosts an annual international inter-religious conference. In Syria – where John Paul II in 2001 became the first pope to step inside a mosque – is the tomb of John the Baptist. On the occupied West Bank, Palestinians are fiercely proud to be Palestinians, whether Muslim or Christian; and Muslims are as likely to be excited about Christians in Bethlehem as the descendants of the first witnesses to the Incarnation. In Egypt, churches, mosques and synagogues jostle against one another – not always without tension, but usually in warm mutual respect and cooperation.

We should therefore not be surprised that in the 1940s, when the Nazis overran North Africa, Arabs sheltered Jews, welcoming them into their homes, sharing their meagre rations with them, and guarding their valuables so the Nazis could not confiscate them. These stories, based on scores of interviews with survivors in the 2,000-year-old Jewish communities of Morocco, Algeria, Tunisia, and Libya, have recently been collected by Robert Satloff, who runs the Washington Institute for Near East Policy. The same can be said of the well documented heroic actions of the Bulgarian people during World War Two when Christians and Muslims alike protected the Jews from similar Nazi persecution. It sometimes takes patient detective work to truffle out these very ordinary, very human tales of people embracing each other. Pieced together, they destroy the poisonous myth of religions at odds with each other.

That myth is no more true nowadays than it was in the past. There may be greater insecurity now, and perhaps a greater willingness to believe the myth, but my broad experience of the Arab world and my charitable work in Britain have taught me quite the opposite story. Who ever hears, for example, of the annual inter-religious conference in Qatar, which this year will invite scholars from around the world to discuss religious and civil rights, freedom of speech and religion, and the role of religion, women and family?

How to explain, for example, one fundraising initiative I was involved with recently? For one year, from June 2004, an Israeli Jew, an Iranian Jew, a French Muslim, a British Protestant and a British and German Catholic came together to fund a Vatican charitable project in mostly Orthodox Serbia and Montenegro. The goodwill and understanding that this generated left a lasting impression on all those involved – donors and recipients alike. It was an everyday story of faith co-operation and understanding - and sadly un-newsworthy.

It is a genuine challenge, in today's climate, to make such collaboration novel and interesting. Yet perhaps we should be reassured by the persistence of news stories about tensions between faiths. News must, after all, be surprising and paradoxical. If inter-religious conflict were the norm, it would cease to be news.

Learning to tell the story of religious coexistence is not a panacea, but is a vital ingredient in achieving a more stable, secure world. Placed in the volatile mix of contemporary politics, the myths of perpetual antagonism have the potential to undo us. We need to keep reminding ourselves – and others – that the tradition of dialogue and coexistence is not just richer and healthier, but much more truthful too.

I am drawn to projects which lead to greater understanding between people divided by religion or identity, projects which defuse tensions and lead to a recognition of what people have in common. That, in essence, is what reconciliation is about. It's a conversion of heart and mind, a revelation of common humanity obscured by the lie of rivalry and antagonism.

Interfaith projects are not, as some believe, abstract theological exchanges, but human relationships built on a common self-interest which lead to the discovery of shared values. Once misunderstandings and fears are cleared away, the common denominator is soon revealed. People stop seeing themselves as rivals, with conflicting self-interests, and start to work together for the good that they have discovered they both believe in. This is, primarily, a work of faith. Children of God seek each other out naturally, as relatives do at a gathering.

People often assume that conflicts between religions arise out of religious differences. In reality, the opposite is true. People of faith have more in common with each other *because* they are religious. The word religion comes from the Latin *ligare* – what binds people together. Religion is, essentially, a force for unity; it is the energy of co-existence. Where religion becomes caught in the net of national identity or political ideology, then conflicts arise between groups – but these are not religious conflicts. Protestants and Catholics were not fighting each other in Northern Ireland over questions of transubstantiation, any more than Israelis and Palestinians kill each other because they disagree over the revelation to the Prophet Muhammad. The problem in each case is that the common bond made possible by religion has been subsumed by rivalry over land or resources. Reconciliation can only happen when these rivalries are dealt with; but overcoming rivalry has to start from somewhere. That "somewhere" is that which supersedes loyalty to nation, race and class – namely faith. Which is why, to paraphrase a very old beer advert, faith reaches the parts that ideology cannot reach.

I have led and participated in many inter-religious events and delegations across Europe and the Arab world which brought together, sometimes for the first time, religious, civil and state leaders from very different backgrounds. It's amazing what can be achieved when people are gathered into one room around a table. Sharing fellowship, dialoguing as equals, experiencing what mainstream Christians call 'communion' – this is the bread-and-butter business of peace and reconciliation.

Western countries sometimes assume, arrogantly, that inter-religious co-operation is the fruit of the secular Enlightenment, and that we should export our models of tolerance to parts of the world which seem in need of them. But we forget that inter-religious co-existence is a new phenomenon in the West, the product of mass immigration in the latter half of the twentieth century, while in many parts of the Middle East and North Africa it is old hat. European countries are struggling to accommodate religious "minorities" within a secular Christian culture, whereas some Middle Eastern cities offer a model of cohabitation and integration we can still only dream of. Compare Damascus – where Christians and Muslims live cheek-by-jowl, thoroughly Syrian all – with parts of Bradford or Birmingham, where Islamic or Hindu communities are often closed in on themselves, alienated from each other and from the society around them. We need to also learn from the Middle East and North Africa, not regard it solely - against the evidence on the ground - as an area waiting for western enlightenment.

Inter-faith dialogue and common action are breaking down these walls. A lodestar in this field was Pope John Paul II, who in 1986 memorably called together the leaders of the world's faiths for a summit in Assisi to pray together for peace – a peace which can only be achieved by addressing the root causes of alienation and resentment.

Twenty-five miles north of Assisi is another town which was the site in the thirteenth century of one of St Francis's classic acts of peacemaking. According to the fable, no doubt embellished in the retelling, there was a wolf who once stalked the woods around the town, preying on its citizens. Francis, visiting Gubbio, heard about the wolf, left the town by the Roman gate, and crossed a large area strewn with human bones, towards the forest, while the people of Gubbio shouted at him to return inside the town walls. When the wolf ran out of the woods and towards Francis, baring its fangs, the saint stood his ground and commanded it in the name of Christ to cease doing harm. The wolf lay down at Francis's feet and, after listening to his peace terms, signalled its agreement to them by placing its paw in the saint's right hand.

This story is sometimes told piously, as if the wolf was suborned by a magic elixir, with St Francis as a sort of shaman. But note that Francis comes from the outside, unarmed, without any agenda or vested interest except peace with justice -- the truly religious agenda. He starts from the assumption that no one can be defined as so barbarian or evil as not to deserve even a word; and he embarks on a dialogue which the townspeople see initially as madness and possibly treason. With the empathy that comes from prayer, Francis also comprehends what lies at the root of the violence (a wolf's appetite being proverbial), and promises his hairy interlocutor that as long as he lived he would make sure he was provided for. And so, for two years afterwards, the redeemed beast made itself at home in Gubbio, going from door to door and being fed by the townspeople. To this day the town's famous quadruped is remembered with a statue.

The faiths are called upon, today, to follow Francis's example in dealing with the new wolves which stalk our world. Injustice, grievance and resentment may sometimes adopt religious clothing, but they are not the result of faith but hunger and anger. The contribution of the religions of the world to addressing these causes is so massive that it is all too easily overlooked. Churches, synagogues, mosques and temples are central to the lives of the very poor around the world: educating them, feeding them, binding their wounds, organising them, bringing them hope, protecting them, standing up for them, and picking them up when they are down. The religious networks of the world are vast channels of solidarity, redistributing wealth and resources to a far greater extent – and with much more immediate effects – than do charities and banks. This presence allows the faiths increasingly to act as partners with international institutions such as UNICEF, the IMF, the World Bank, the Commonwealth and to put pressure on the wealthiest nations to meet the Millennium Development Goals. Wherever human beings are held back by HIV/Aids, drug-fuelled violence, unemployment, discrimination, or lack of opportunity, the faiths are there, confronting the challenges and setting people free.

The great twentieth-century international political institutions have failed to stem the tides of conflict; could it now be the turn of the religions? Faiths increasingly need to be mobilised for peace, because peace can only be brought about by transcending self-interest: the one God of all to those of faith and not just the global marketplace or universal charters of rights. As Pope John Paul said in the second meeting at Assisi, in 2002, an association of religion with nationalistic, political and economic interests or concerns of other kinds is "unjustified" by the nature of religion itself. When religions are allowed to fall either side of these divides, glaring at each other over their scriptures, we are all the losers. Hence the urgent need for dialogue between religions to counteract the human dynamic which drives wedges between them. The faiths are being called, now, to take centre stage as the agent of peace in the world, to listen carefully to each other, sensitive to any instance of a faith community profiting from the injustice which oppresses another, to hear each other's hunger and seek to respond to it.

What are my hopes for the future of inter-faith dialogue in this country and abroad? It is perhaps summed up in a story I heard some time ago: A Rabbi asked his disciples to define that moment we call dawn when the morning prayers may be said. One disciple said very reasonably: 'It is dawn when you can tell a horse from a donkey.' Another said: 'Ah, yes, but that is not good enough- it is dawn when you can tell an olive tree from a fig tree.' And the rest all offered their best guesses. At last the Rabbi said: 'You are all correct. But for the dawn that really matters it will be sunrise when you can look a stranger in the face and see your sister or your brother.'

Of course, there are many encouragements but we must learn how to tell the story of it happening so that it can happen more. For it is essential work, in both senses of that word: the work is vital, and it is in the essence of faith to carry it out. Where the faiths work together, the benefits are multiplied indefinitely; peace and justice break out, and the world moves closer to what it is intended to be.

HE Anthony Bailey, KCSS, is Chairman of the Faith Task Force of the Labour Party and Chief Policy Adviser to the Board of Directors of the Foreign Policy Centre. He is an established inter-faith campaigner and holds senior posts with the Three Faiths Forum, the King Faisal Foundation, the Maimonides Foundation, Sacred Military Constantinian Order of St George and the Foundation of Reconciliation and Relief in the Middle East. He is also a member of two Ministerial Task Forces at the Department of Education and Skills.

Military Intervention from a Christian Perspective

Lord Harries of Pentregarth

I strongly opposed the current war in Iraq. But if only I had been proved wrong. If only it had proved possible to remove Saddam Hussein without all the terrible suffering that has in fact ensued. I would willingly have been prepared to look foolish, as I am sure would everyone else who opposed the war. One of my worries about the present terrible debacle is that it might discredit the whole idea of military intervention on behalf of those who are being oppressed. For I believe that in the modern world the international community should, under certain circumstances, intervene to stop appalling things happening. I supported the 1993 Gulf War to expel Saddam Hussein from Kuwait and long urged intervention to prevent atrocities in Bosnia and Kosovo. So I am not a pacifist. Like most, though not all, Christians, I believe that sometimes there is a duty to use force. The phrase "Just War" is an unfortunate one. It implies justice is all on one side. Often it isn't and war is always a tragedy, fought with a sense of sadness as the lesser of two evils. This distinguishes the Christian Just War tradition from the crusade mentality, which assumes a war is being fought on behalf of God against God's enemies. You can never assume that. All you can do is make the best human judgement you can and the criteria of the Just War tradition are there to help.

Some think these criteria have been outmoded by modern warfare and technology. They have not. For, even if you judge a particular war wrong, as I did the current Iraq war, it will be by using particular criteria and these will almost certainly be closely related if not identical to those provided by the developed tradition of Christian thinking on the subject. Indeed these criteria have recently received a remarkable tribute. A recent high powered UN report came up with criteria for military intervention which are almost identical to those of the Just War tradition.[47]

The first criterion for military intervention is that there must be lawful authority. Until recently this has had to be the government of a nation state because there has been no higher international authority to which appeal could be made. But now we have the United Nations. The present UN may be weak and flawed, but that makes it all the more urgent that we take it seriously and try to make it better and stronger. Of course national self interest is present in the UN, as it is in all international bodies. But it provides a context in which these interests can be negotiated to find a consensus that is truly in the interest of international order and justice.

The second criterion is that there must be a just cause. Gross violation of human rights and genocide is certainly such a cause. A major debate at the moment is whether pre-emptive intervention is ever justified. Suppose it is known for certain that a country is developing weapons of mass destruction, that there are gross human rights violations taking place within its borders and that it has a record of attacking its neighbours, could it be right to attack it before it actually acquired those weapons? It could be, but only on the authorisation of the UN, for otherwise it would be all to easy for states to intervene in other countries without an adequate reason for doing so; disguising national self-interest with talk about security.

Thirdly, every effort must have been made to resolve an issue by peaceful means. War must be a last resort when every other avenue has been explored. Of course it might not be possible to leave the matter right to the very last moment, because by then the tyranny might have done untold damage and taken such hold it could not be dislodged or only dislodged at terrible cost. A balance has to be struck between trying all peaceful means and other considerations. It would have been possible to have gone

---

[47] 'A more secure world: our shared responsibility', Report of the UN High-Level Panel on Threats, Challenges and Change, December 2004

on negotiating for years over the Falklands through the UN. In that case we would have to accept the fact that the Falklands would almost certainly still be in Argentinean hands. That might have been a right outcome, but we should not hide the realities.

Fourthly, it must be judged that the evil unleashed by the military intervention will not outweigh the possible good. This is of course a particularly difficult judgement to make but it must be made. For example, there could be a manifest wrong in a particular country but trying to put it right might do more harm than good. In such a case military intervention would be wrong.

Fifthly, there must be a reasonable chance of success. For obviously it would be wrong to intervene if there was no chance of rectifying the evil. It is important to probe the question about what counts for success in any particular situation. In counter-terrorism, for example, it is not a matter of winning great military battles, though force is likely to have to be used. Counter-terrorism is primarily a matter of good intelligence and winning hearts and minds. If this is lost sight of, things can go badly wrong.

Each of these criteria raise questions and they cannot be applied in a wooden way. Difficult judgements have to be made, and it is always possible for those who make them to be blinded by considerations of narrow national interest. But unless those criteria are met no intervention could be morally justified.

Sadly, we live in a world where there are still, and are likely to be in the future, gross violations of human rights in some countries and perhaps places where whole peoples are under threat. It is vital that the international community acts in such circumstances. The terrible tragedy of the Iraq War must not have the effect of making it impossible to get international support for military action in such circumstances. But the key issue is to strengthen the United Nations and enable it to have both the confidence of its member states and the resources to do the difficult jobs it will be called on to do. For military intervention to be right it must be seen to be right; seen to be right by the body most able to judge that such action is needed for the common good and is not just an expression of the aggrandisement of a particular nation.

The Rt Rev Richard Harries, Lord Harries of Pentregarth, is the former Bishop of Oxford. He was previously the Dean of King's College London and a founder member of the Oxford Abrahamic Group, bringing together Christian, Muslim, and Jewish scholars.

The impact of the Israel/Palestine conflict on Muslim-Jewish relations in the UK

Dr Richard Stone

A microcosm of the impact of Israel/Palestine in the UK

At a time of intensification of Israeli retaliation against Palestinian retaliation, the Islamic Society (ISoc) of a major UK university is so incensed that it proposes a motion to the student Union entitled 'Palestinian Human Rights'. This condemns Zionism, as well as Israeli policies against Palestinians. The Jewish Society (JSoc) is angry that there is no mention of Palestinian suicide bombing. The JSoc opposes the motion, which by declaring Zionism as racist, would result in a banning of the JSoc which, as a Zionist organisation, will be deemed racist.

The heated debate is reminiscent of Montagus and Capulets, with young men on each side swearing and spitting at each other. Behind the men, two women exchange glances across the floor in ways which show that they are in despair of these "boys stamping their feet in the playground". The Muslim student is active in the Isoc; she has Palestinian friends, and she does not have a problem with the motion itself. She connects with a Jewish woman and they agree "there has to be a better way than this". They set up a dialogue group with other women friends which meets three times a term for over two years.

As so often, peace starts with women. The group moves swiftly away from aggressive "boys in the playground" stuff. They are into serious dynamic and constructive exchanges on topics which really matter to them: the role of women in patriarchal religions; comparisons of observance and non-observance of religious practices; employment opportunities for women graduates and the glass ceilings that they face; women writers in English literature, poetry, art and so on.

This is a private, closed group of people who develop warm and close friendships. In due time they get round to studying the Qur'an and the later scholars' commentaries. This is in tandem with the Torah and its later rabbinic comments, so they feel that they can now call themselves an 'interfaith group'. Yet much of what they do is actually 'inter-community', but between two communities which identify themselves by their religious backgrounds.

At another time and place, a student group attends a meeting of *Alif-Aleph UK (British Muslims - British Jews)*. "We badly need advice. If we talk about the Israel/Palestine conflict we will fall apart. But if we don't talk about it we will fall apart. What can we do?"

The larger political impact

It is generally accepted that taught history is that of the victors in any conflict. The history of the vanquished survives, if at all, as part of the victimhood of generations of the vanquished.

In the Israel/Palestine conflict there have been five or more wars since the founding of the Israeli state in 1948, and grumbling conflict between Jews and Palestinians for 100 years, even before the Balfour Declaration of 1917. With no resolution neither side is the victor, and the narratives of each have become polished and polarised, with each side pointing the finger at the alleged faults of the other. These are then used as ammunition in a war of words which always blames the other side for failure to make peace.

In the UK, on the North-West fringes of Europe, there is no political reason whatever for Muslims and Jews to do other than rebuild together a Golden Age as they did in 13th century Andalusia and in 18th century Salonika. Maybe those Golden Ages were not all that Golden, but for both communities the conditions then were, sad to say, better than both of their negative experiences of Christian Europe.

A major problem is low levels of knowledge about the issues. Few on both sides know much about the Golden Ages. There is considerable ignorance of the recent histories of Israel and Palestine, in particular of the many positive contacts and active joint projects over there which have been maintained even during the Second Intifada and the recent Lebanon war. The facts of the establishment of the Israeli State, and Jewish and Palestinian experiences are taught almost entirely from the view of one side or the other.

In Europe today there are significant communities of Muslims and Jews living side by side but few recognise that this is a totally new situation for both. In the past Jews living next door to Muslims were always "Dhimmi" (second class citizens) under Muslim rule. Now both communities are minorities in secular/Christian Europe. For a growing handful of Muslims and Jews this is seen as an opportunity which is being developed with dramatic and positive results.

For the leadership of both communities such positive activity is almost impossible to maintain because of the looming impact of the unresolved Israel/Palestine conflict. The established leaders on both sides take on the natural affinity for co-religionists involved in a desperate struggle 2,500 miles away, and bristle with aggressive and defensive rhetoric which can often be worse than that heard in the Middle East itself.

For Anglo-Jewry it is hard to do anything other than leap to the defence of Israel where 5 million Jews are 80% of the population, but less than 50% of the population of Israel and the Palestinian territories combined. Muslim leadership in the UK is naturally drawn to supporting the Palestinians, about 90% of whom are Muslims. Incidentally, almost no-one talks these days about the 400,000 or so Christians who inhabited the land 60 years ago, and are probably now less than 100,000.

Many British Muslims and British Jews in private freely express their distress for the plight of "ordinary people" on both sides and they support the concept of a Two-State Solution, though expressing despair at how either side will get there. However, such are the entrenched positions of the leaderships and media of each community that it has become almost impossible to express in public any disagreement with the established "Israel right or wrong" and "Palestine right or wrong" stances.

Jonathan Freedland, the Guardian (Jewish) journalist wrote in 2006 that he felt he "inhabits a tiny sliver of land" squeezed by the defensive Jewish establishment on one side and pro-Palestinian Jews on the other.

The recent launch of a 'Declaration' by a new group calling itself 'Independent Jewish Voices' (IJV) was met by an outcry of "you are Jew-hating Jews, who do nothing as Jews except to attack and undermine Israel" – this despite a few signatories being Jews who are active in mainstream Jewish society.

For many Jews the whole IJV Declaration was ill conceived. For others, while it expressed acceptable even-handed support for both sides of the Israel/Palestine conflict, they feel they could not sign because so many of the signatories were too well known as unacceptable to the mainstream Jewish establishment. These 'middle path' non-signatories did not want to lose friends in British Jewry. Yet more did not sign because they are determined to keep their lines open with both sides within the Jewish community, hopefully to bridge increasing divisions between those seen as either pro-Israel or anti-Israel. Sadly, it can sometimes be hard to argue for support in public for the Human Rights of both Israelis and Palestinians.

As chair of the reconvened Islamophobia Commission, set up originally by the Runnymede Trust 1995-97, I found little concern in the early phases (up to 2004) that I was also chair of the Jewish Council for Racial Equality. I was seen, I think, as "Dr Stone, the non-Muslim concerned with Islamophobia who happens to be a Jew". For most Muslims this appeared to be an asset, though I sensed very occasional hostility from a few individuals.

However it has been different this year. I am much more often "Dr Stone, the Jew who chairs the Commission". Yet it was at the request of several Muslim colleagues at the Home Office's 2005/06 'Preventing Extremism Together' Working Groups that I got into reconvening for a third phase. It has taken a year to sort out that there really is a need for a group of Muslims and non-Muslims to work alongside the burgeoning British Muslim voluntary sector. It has also taken sensitivity and a lot of listening around the country to set it up in a way that respects the effectiveness of Muslim organisations and does not duplicate their initiatives. The Commission seeks out gaps and facilitates appropriate filling of them.

This time I have felt more resentment somehow linked to my Jewish identity. During the second Intifada and again during the recent Lebanon war, there has been an expectation by some people that I can only be "a proper friend of British Muslims" if I publicly criticise Israeli actions against Palestinians.

Advice from Muslim colleagues is to ignore these pressures. "The strength of the Commission has always been that it works in this country, on issues that affect Muslims in this country". "Don't be swayed by those who want to drag you into international politics, which are not really your field. Stick to what you know about (the experience of British Muslims) and have been doing for the last 10 years".

Conflict in the Middle East spills over to divide Jews from Muslims in this country. It also divides Jew from Jew, as it divides Muslim from Muslim.

Attempts are being made by numerous Muslim individuals and organisations to get out a more nuanced response to Israel/Palestine than what is reported in the media as 'the response of Muslims'. Frustration is often heard that "we are not one community with one response. To almost any issue we have lots of different responses, just like other communities whose pluralities are given more respect".

During the 2000/04 phase of the Commission I was asked to lead a delegation to a British newspaper to complain of its anti-Palestinian (and anti-Muslim) bias. A few months earlier, a delegation from the Board of Deputies of British Jews had visited the same paper about bias against Israel (and against Jews). Needless to say, it was not for me to mention the Board's problems during the Islamophobia Commission visit. The journalists seemed rather puzzled.

Part of the problem is that the Israel/Palestine history is polarised into two (if not more) narratives. There is an urgent need for education about the histories set out in ways which do not exacerbate tensions. Any mere're-writing' of a single new version is bound to be challenged by each side as 'distorting the truth'. However, in 1978 a Young Fabian pamphlet set out the Palestinian and the Israeli narratives side by side. The Islamophobia Commission plans to update this pamphlet as one its series of pamphlets in 2007/08.

It is hoped that this pamphlet, with another on 'the positive contribution of Muslims & Islam to Britain', and another on 'the history of Islamophobia in Britain', will empower more Muslims to speak out with authority on issues that concern them. Maybe this will overcome the diffidence of the many who as yet feel unable to challenge official Muslim and non-Muslim statements with which they disagree.

There is an increasing recognition that those who keep their status in mainstream Muslim and Jewish community organisations, while retaining their credibility with their community's 'independents', could be well placed to facilitate joint Muslim-Jewish work with Parliamentarians and diplomats on foreign affairs, and on domestic 'Cohesion'.

The role of British diaspora support for each side of the Israel/Palestine conflict was recognised by Israeli and Palestinian governments at a Ditchley Park conference a few years ago. Senior Palestinian and Israeli delegates made a joint plea for British Governmental facilitation of the peace process: the UN,

USA and EU were no longer trusted by both sides. Whether this was posturing or a genuine belief that Britain is the nearest to a neutral significant outsider has to be decided by the FCO.

The hope has to be that British Muslims and British Jews recognise the benefits of working together in this country – as many already do. Each does its best to lobby for its own community, and to bring peace for Israel/Palestine through its own lobbying groups such as Parliamentary Friends of Israel or Parliamentary Middle East Councils. However lobbying is bound to be more effective if these Muslim and Jewish lobbies can find common ground to do it together.

In the April '07 Progress magazine, David Pinto-Duschinsky advocates "dialogue with moderate Islamic parties" in the Middle East as a way to "persuade, aid and pressure our non-democratic allies to open up their societies". This is his recipe to avoid the inevitable "long term chaos" which is likely to result from short-run support for the status quo.

I would refine his general working "with moderate Islamic parties" to "seeking individuals within Islamic parties who are open to flexibility". No political party is a homogeonous group of utterly like-minded people. There are always hard-liners and more open people in even the most radical party. The British FCO has a tradition of seeking out these individuals in all groupings seen to be hostile to UK interests . What better team could our FCO field for this delicate task than one led by a small group of British Muslims & British Jews, perhaps including some parliamentarians, who have developed trust and experience together?

To reach such a position, help from outside (eg FCO and DCLG) is needed. It is not enough just to facilitate Muslims and Jews to meet. The help needs to go further and support those who attempt to build bridges between the factions within each community so that there will be alliances within each which can engage with alliances in the other. Leaving this task to 'mainstream' community leadership organisations has not been as productive as one would have hoped, given the current state of turmoil 2,500 miles away.

Old and new voices in UK Muslim-Jewish dialogue make similar pleas for outside support from British government Ministers, not just in the FCO and DCLG but also in the Home Office, DfES, and other relevant departments. They are shy to ask for help for those who are into building bridges between 'mainstream leadership' and the 'independent' voices outside it, partly because they sense that (for them) Government leans too much towards established leadership only.

Parallels with community divisions in Northern Ireland are obvious. Potential resolution of conflict between British Muslims and British Jews, and between Israelis and Palestinians seems to come most often from joint action between women on both sides who cry "a plague on both your houses".

This brings us back to what happened to the student group which feared collapse whatever option it took on discussing Israel/Palestine. An experienced Imam and I offered some suggestions on how to address the issue, and the women disappeared off to their campus.

Only a year later did the group report that they had "talked about talking about Israel/Palestine" on two occasions. "Then it didn't seem so important any more to talk about it!" "We were suffering from free floating anxiety... Actually, we have another question: we are in our last undergraduate year, and we want the group to continue after we have gone. How can we make that happen?"

That led to discussions on the role of a relatively experienced central group in inter-community facilitation. *Alif-Aleph UK* can seek a Muslim and a Jew from the college staff, or from the local mainstream community, who are prepared to take on a mentoring role. There will usually be little for them to do except at the beginning of each academic year when they could invite the surviving members from the previous year for tea and cake, and be there for them later as they take on the leadership. *Alif-*

Aleph UK has put these senior names into its database, with an action command each September to email the mentors to remind them to invite in the new leaders.

The message is plain: the myriad positive contacts between British Muslims and British Jews give hope of building bridges for a better Britain and for a better Middle East.

Dr Richard Stone is the founder and President of Alif-Aleph UK (British Muslims and British Jews). He is the Chair of the Islamophobia Commission (set up by the Runnymede Trust in 1995) and President of the Jewish Council for Racial Equality. Dr Stone was a panel member of the Stephen Lawrence Inquiry as Adviser to Sir William Macpherson.

The War on terror – not just an issue for Muslims

Sunny Hundal

Four days after the atrocities of September 11th 2001, a gas-station owner in Mesa, Arizona, was shot and killed by an American man claiming it was in retaliation to the terrorist attack. The turban and full beard may have given him away but 52 year-old Balbir Singh Sodhi was not of Muslim but Sikh faith and the first such victim. Many more victims of racial harassment were to follow.

The 'War on Terror' (WoT) has never been an issue just for British Muslims. Bubbling underneath the national conversation around Islamist groups, anti-terror legislation and civil rights, a change has been taking place within minority communities in the way they interact with each other, identify themselves and become politically engaged.

The terrorist attacks of 9/11 and 7/7 inevitably exacerbated tensions between British Muslim, Sikh and Hindu families who lived in close proximity to each other. This has been reflected not only in local events but on a wider national level. It has also fuelled a drive towards faith-based identity while discarding the old solidarity-based identity politics of race.

It is vital for the Labour government to not only understand this shift in identity politics but be aware of the dangers of being sucked into them and compromise its own social cohesion agenda. It is also possible, despite the currently muddled discourse, to spearhead a much needed national conversation around citizenship, democratic engagement and better race relations, to help build a more cosmopolitan Britain in the 21st century.

A changing identity

Not long after 9/11 a group of Sikhs from around the country organised a vigil outside the American embassy in London to reiterate that 'Sikhs were not Muslims' in an attempt to distance themselves from the latter. It was mostly in response to the hate-crimes that followed 9/11, but partly fuelled by faith groups eager to assert their own religious identity.

In January 2002 Sunrise Radio, a popular station in west London, capitulated to pressure from hard-line Sikh and Hindu groups and stopped using the term 'Asian'. It was designed to avoid putting them in the same category as British Muslims. Although the station later backtracked, the damage was done.

In the same year some extremist members of the Sikh gang *Shere Punjab* even allied themselves with the British National Party. The attempt to create an alliance against Muslims had little political impact but the BNP was undeterred, employing the same strategy in 2005 by using a Sikh man in their party political broadcast.

The atmosphere of distrust following 9/11 and 7/7 made it easier for Muslim, Sikh and Hindu religious extremists to openly express distaste towards other religious minorities. Groups such as Al-Muhajiroun[48] published leaflets calling for Sikh and Hindu girls to be converted and brought into the fold of Islam, and organised events in central London openly berating other religions and calling for more conversions.

A documentary on BBC Asian Network radio station late last year titled 'Don't Call Me Asian'[49] laid out the divide in stark terms, citing statements from Hindu and Sikh organisations who wanted to discard the term Asian as a means to distance themselves from Muslims.

---

[48] Then led by Sheikh Omar Bakri, Al-Muhajiround was an off-shoot of the Islamist group Hizb ut-Tahrir. It has since materialised under different names.
[49] www.bbc.co.uk/asiannetwork/documentaries/dontcallmeasian.shtml

The presenter asks: "But are they saying 'don't call me Asian' because the term is meaningless, or are they saying 'don't associate me with Muslims, because the movement against the term Asian is aimed at distancing themselves from Muslims in the eyes of the media, the politicians and the population at large."

New community leaders

Although other factors have also influenced the shift towards faith identity, notably conflict in the Middle East and South-Asia[50], the upshot has been the emergence and increased visibility of religious "community leaders". The Labour party has no doubt played a part in the process, facilitating the development of the Muslim Council of Britain, which led to copycat initiatives from the Hindu and Sikh communities.

But whereas earlier campaigners for equality and anti-racism from minority communities came largely from a secular and progressive-left background, emphasising solidarity and unity, the new generation bring with them a conservative-right brand of politics with an emphasis on religious segregation.

Although a great deal of light has been shed on the ideological influences and background of the members that drive the Muslim Council of Britain[51] much less has been said of its counterparts such as the Sikh Federation UK and Hindu Forum of Britain, who are even more secretive of their agenda.

The Sikh Federation UK's leadership is primarily composed of members from the International Sikh Youth Federation, which was banned in the UK in March 2001 for suspected terrorist

---

[50] The Gujarat riots of 2002 also antagonised relations between British Hindus and Muslims
[51] John Ware's Panorama programme: 'A Question of Leadership' and Martin Bright's report 'When Progressives Treat With Reactionaries'.

activity in India. Although the body was disbanded, its members were free to set themselves up under a different name.

The Hindu Forum of Britain meanwhile shares ideological roots with the RSS (*Rashtriya Swayamsevak Sangh,* in India*)* and is affiliated with VHP-UK (an arm of Vishwa Hindu Parishad in India) both hardline Hindu militant organisations that are part of the same umbrella.

Given that the RSS is deeply distrusted both by Sikhs (for their activities in the Indian state of Punjab) and Muslims (for its role in the anti-Muslim pogroms in Gujarat state in 2002), all these organisations are ideologically opposed to each other.

The desire for identity separation at national level is closely linked to a grab for government funding and political influence. This in turn has sparked competition between faith-based organisations for attention, creating a perverse incentive for them to adopt a victim mentality and build controversies where they can thrust themselves into the media limelight as representatives of a community under attack.[52]

Sikh and Hindu groups constantly stress[53] the need to become more vocal about demanding their share of funding and government support even when it isn't made clear what that money will be used for.

The new Britishness

Given this context the government faces huge challenges. It needs to deal with home-grown terrorism and religious extremism while ensuring the vast majority of innocent Muslims are not alienated by its policies. But as political multiculturalism has come to the forefront since the WoT, i.e. the prominence

---

[52] Two examples covered in the national media include the banning of the Sikh play Behzti in Christmas 2004, and the Hindu Royal Mail stamp controversy.
[53] Eastern Eye newspaper, 6th October 2006.
www.easterneyeonline.co.uk/iframe_story.asp?NID=4107

given to Muslim bodies such as the MCB, it has indirectly encouraged Sikh and Hindu groups to make similar demands

Labour needs to reiterate its commitment to secularism and lay out guidelines for engagement with such groups, treating them as lobby groups as opposed to representative bodies.

On areas such as education for example it should consult with a wide range of scholars when formulating policy rather than simply the ones offered by such organisations. The alternative is that each body will seek to influence government agenda by offering experts that conform to their conservative views, putting more obstacles in the way of social cohesion and accusing the government of bias if their view is ignored.

Events since 9/11 have also presented the government with an opportunity to have a debate on modern Britain. There has always been a pervasive feeling amongst minority groups that their contribution has never really been recognised or appreciated; that they remain invisible in the national cultural and political conversation.

With the Muslim community now thrust into the limelight, their aspirations, interests and ideas discussed like never before, Labour can use this opportunity to create an informed debate on issues around 'Britishness', democracy and free speech.

While discarding the old politics of 'take me to your leader', it needs to emphasise a common thread of citizenship based on local civic participation, social duty and building relationships with national institutions - for all Britons.

The War on Terror has undoubtedly lead to British Asians asserting their religiosity more aggressively. This is not a problem in itself since religious identity need not trump a more national identity. Indeed most young ethnic minorities are commonly found to be comfortable living with multiple identities.

The trick is to allow a private space where those identities can be manifested while ensuring a public space where national identity is promoted and people are recognised only on that basis. Pandering to groups along ethnic or religious lines will inevitably create tension and foster competition between organisations.

The government has to push a message that says every Briton has an equal part to play in improving society or making their voice heard without focusing too much on their differences.

That is an agenda not just for Muslims but all Britons.

Sunny Hundal spearheaded the launch of New Generation Network last year, a group set up to challenge the current discourse of race and faith relations in the UK. He has written for most broadsheets on related issues. He is also editor of Asians in Media magazine and runs the progressive 'Pickled Politics' blog.

Faith, Human Rights and the Question of Universalism - A Case Study of Freedom of Thought, Conscience and Religion

Daniel Wheatley

"All human beings are born free and equal in dignity and rights."
From article one, The Universal Declaration of Human Rights

The first article of the Universal Declaration of Human Rights reminds us of the moral and philosophical bedrock of our emerging rights culture, that we are all equal. In the early days of the twenty first century (Christian Era) many would take such an assertion for granted. Yet it is not so very long ago that throughout the world it was common practice for states to give legal expression to discrimination by race, caste or class. Even today there are still clear examples of laws and practices that demote women to second class status. Great progress has been made since 1948 but the vision of full human rights for every citizen of our evermore interdependent planet remains far from fulfilled.

This proclamation of the inalienable equality of human beings matches closely with the moral code that members of the Baha'i faith derive from the core principles of their faith; the oneness of humanity, the inherent nobility of the human creation and the primacy of justice in the eyes of the God that Baha'is believe in. Commenting on this drive towards human unity in 2002 the global governing body of the Baha'i faith, the Universal House of Justice, observed that, *"The enduring legacy of the twentieth century is that it compelled the peoples of the world to begin seeing themselves as the members of a single human race..."*

Baha'is in the UK and our 5- 6 million co-religionists around the world are clear, however, that this optimistic and integrative process is far from complete. The development of a conception of equality and dignity into the substantive realisation of rights for all members of the human race must co-exist with and struggle against the forces of disintegration in our world. Forces that divide humanity and promulgate a spectrum of doctrines of discrimination and intolerance militate against the advance of universal human rights. As a community of belief, it pains us to acknowledge that, tragically, organised religion behaves all too frequently as one of the most formidable obstacles in the path of human unity and felicity.

At a time of growing controversies over the language and nature of human rights, compounded by concerns over practices that are regarded by many as taking either an exceptionalist or a relativist approach to rights set out in the Universal Declaration and subsequently codified into core international conventions, it is appropriate to revisit one of the fundamental questions within this debate: are human rights universal?

The Baha'i community internationally has, of necessity, had to develop a level of expertise in the specific area of freedom of thought, conscience and religion in order to defend Baha'i minorities in several states where they face persecution from the state on grounds of their spiritual beliefs. Whilst it is sadly true that vast numbers of people continue to endure the effects of ingrained prejudices of ethnicity, gender, nation, caste and class, any objective study of the last century of human societies would have to concede that at the level of the global discourse such concepts as the equality of the sexes, and the rejection of racial and ethnic prejudices have largely assumed the force of universally accepted principles.

It is the contention of this short essay, however, that such progress has not been made in the field of religious tolerance and that the suggestion that all of the world's great religions are equally valid is stubbornly resisted by entrenched patterns of sectarian thought. For those outside the religious fold the assertion of atheist or secular convictions in some parts of the world can face similar resistance. The right to investigate beliefs for oneself and to change one's religion or belief, as envisioned in article 18 of the Universal Declaration, has been weakened in the language of subsequent international instruments, and those struggling for freedom of religion or belief, lack the support of a separate convention with the backing of a UN treaty-monitoring committee, as is provided for such other areas of rights such as racial discrimination or discrimination against women. It is no surprise, therefore, to see growing evidence in the world of intolerance and persecution motivated by reason of divisive dogmas, including those that are religious in nature and insist on claims of sole access to spiritual truth, but also by atheistic systems that deny human beings the freedom of the life of the mind and the right to investigate truth for themselves and to practice a religion of their own choosing. The international system has less in its tool-kit to address issues of religious intolerance.

In this brief piece the author wishes to explore the question of the universalism of human rights and to explore this issue through the case-study of freedom of religion or belief.

The Baha'i faith emerged as an independent religious movement out of an Islamic milieu in Iran in the mid nineteenth century. Certain theological claims, foundational to Baha'is' beliefs, are inimical to key tenets of sharia law. Baha'is' acceptance of two spiritual leaders in 19th century Iran as prophets bearing divine messages has been the primary motivation for relentless persecution of Baha'is in Iran at the hands of fundamentalist elements of the Shi'ite clergy and latterly, a policy of state repression by the government since the 1979 revolution.

Faced with executions of over 200 community leaders, the torture and imprisonment of hundreds more of their members, and a wide-range of civil rights denials, such as access to education and expropriation of communal and sacred properties, the Iranian Baha'is turned to the international community for protection. Baha'i representatives at the United Nations made the case for their defence not in theological terms, but in the language of human rights and through the mechanisms of international law. As violence against the Iranian Baha'is mounted in the years immediately after the revolution the international Baha'i community lobbied national governments and international institutions to take appropriate action. From 1983 onwards resolutions at the UN Commission on Human Rights, and then the UN General Assembly, spearheaded a campaign of multi-lateral and bi-lateral efforts to censure Iran's persecution of a peaceful and law-abiding minority. A study of the subsequent trends demonstrates that the killing of Baha'is and other serious violations of rights begins to diminish in number from this period of time, although systematic persecution of the community has continued in many other ways and is now clearly on the rise again.

With over 25 years of collective experience, the Baha'i community has become quite expert in the international machinery of human rights, particularly with respect to the rights of freedom of religion or belief. Our community are both advocates for universal human rights, as a point of religious principle, but are also beneficiaries of these rights. There are many Baha'is who owe their lives to such concepts and the institutions that try to put them into effect, some now living in the UK.

Human rights groups operating at the global level will be familiar with the unfortunate trends that led to the dissolution of the UN Commission on Human Rights. Many factors undermined the credibility of the world's primary forum for the promotion and protection of human rights; the increasing politicisation of the human rights debate and the election to the Commission of states that were accused of egregious rights violations. In earlier years apologists for the abuse of Baha'is had, when facing scrutiny from international rights instruments, argued – unsuccessfully – that human rights represented Western values, and were not universal.

It is profoundly discouraging for those who campaign for human rights to witness the resurgence of the questioning of the universalism of human rights. This has found new forms of expression. The position of many UN member states that they will never vote for criticism of the human rights record of any government abandons defenceless populations to the machinations of the state, as in Darfur, and on closer inspection is often found to be inconsistent with many of the same states' record on human rights advocacy.

This questioning of universalism has been the meta-debate within human rights since the drafting of the Universal Declaration in 1948, and it remains far from a settled matter. The experience of those Baha'i agencies that work on such issues, an experience that we believe will be shared by human rights advocates everywhere, is that the voices of those who face execution for their beliefs, or are tortured and incarcerated by their own governments, do not share the moral relativist argument that human rights are not universal. Indeed, we wonder if there are many human beings who have endured the cruelty of the manifold assaults upon their dignity that are to be found in the baleful spectrum of human rights abuses, who if they are fortunate enough to escape with their lives, do not desire the same rights of life, security, physical integrity, liberty, and freedom of speech that are once again being questioned as the unique privileges of citizens of Western culture?

In the 21st century with all the interconnectedness that arises from the well-documented trends of migration, communications and travel, human values and ideas about how human societies should live flow with increasing velocity through the evermore porous borders of states. Egyptian citizens sitting at computers are fully literate in the language of the rights that the international community asserts are their birthright as members of the human race. Sadly, just as the progressive forces of integration can flow anywhere on earth, negative forces of disintegration also operate globally in a borderless world. For many years the Baha'i community has sought to defend the lives of individuals in Iran who have faced imprisonment and even death for the crime of apostasy, that is to say for having converted from the faith of Islam to another belief. It is deeply worrying and an alarming indicator of the retreat from universalism to hear credible reports in increasing number of people who convert from Islam to Christianity or other faiths facing threats and intimidation in the UK and other Western democracies.

We are unapologetic advocates for universal human rights. We suggest that promoting freedom of religion or belief needs to become a higher priority for policy-makers globally and we would welcome the UK government taking a leadership role in this respect. UK foreign policy could bring to bear its considerable influence at the United Nations to give serious consideration to four critical yet neglected issues:

1. the right to change one's religion or belief
2. the right to share one's belief with others
3. the responsibility of the international community and national governments vis á vis marginalised and peacefully organised religious communities
4. the responsibilities of religious leaders vis á vis marginalised and peacefully organised religious communities

We submit that a danger grows that the rising fires of religious prejudice will ignite a worldwide conflagration, greater yet that the problems that beset the world today, the consequences of which are unthinkable. Efforts to protect human rights, such as freedom of religion or belief, are not merely a legal exercise or pragmatic necessity for certain religious groups. This human right, as much as any other, is part of a larger and essentially spiritual undertaking that will allow human potential to emerge and flourish. These potentialities exist in every human being, in the UK, Iran or anywhere else.

The teachings of the Prophet-Founder of our faith, Baha'u'llah, are clear: the fate of humanity itself is inextricably bound in with the recognition of our undeniable oneness as a single, yet beautifully diverse human species.

> *"The well-being of mankind, its peace and security, are unattainable unless and until its unity is firmly established".*
> Baha'u'llah (1817 – 1892)

Daniel Wheatley is the Government Relations Officer of the Baha'i Community of the UK. The National Spiritual Assembly of the Bahá'ís of the United Kingdom is the elected governing body of members of the Bahá'í faith in the UK.

Defrocking Muslim Women

Urmee Khan

Such a little thing can make such a difference. Growing up in a Muslim household, you get accustomed to the slender pieces of fabric, in miscellaneous designs, handed down by posterity; one among many pieces of personal cultural baggage. The act of putting the veil on never seemed a public and political act – until last year.

It's a truth self evident – though sometimes ignored by specialists – that domestic policy and foreign policy are intrinsically linked, and perhaps more so now than for decades. During the Cold War, foreign policy was a major division between the political parties, but those divisions, whilst deep, were not sociological. Now, however, foreign policy decisions have a direct impact on inter-ethnic relations in Britain. Moreover, there is some evidence that foreign policy is a factor influencing the voting decisions of the general public much more so than in the past: witness almost 2 million protestors who took to London's streets against the Iraq war, and some years ago the million who were mobilised by the churches for Jubilee 2000. Many senior figures have acknowledged the direct link between foreign policy and domestic strife, including the outgoing head of MI5, Dame Eliza Manningham-Buller who has admitted that Britain's foreign policy had helped to alienate and radicalise young Muslim men.

This connection works in the other direction too. It may sound aspirational, but is nevertheless true, that a Britain sure of and at ease with its values can be a beacon in a world where civilisational values are a site of such conflict. Foreign policy is no longer - if it ever was - a private matter discussed by mandarins in Whitehall, but a felt reality on the world's streets.

In this context, a debate which dominated much of 2006, the wearing of veils or other forms of covering by Muslim women, takes on a new potency. At several points in 2005-06 the judicial process in Britain was required to rule on the appropriateness or otherwise of Muslim women's clothes. The Luton teenager Shabina Begum was embroiled in a row over the wearing of Islamic dress in school. Later it was the turn of a teacher, Aishah Azmi from Yorkshire, to be centre of attention over her choice of clothing. In her case, one government minister – Phil Woolas – said that she should be sacked while her industrial tribunal was still on-going; strange behaviour, perhaps, for a former trade union official. Later, lawyer Shabnam Mughal was asked by a senior judge to remove her veil in court. She declined to do so and the case was adjourned on two occasions.

Generally, when there has been an issue over race or ethnic culture, the government of the day is careful not to assert that the issue threatens the very integrity of multiculturalism. But in 2006, Labour ministers embraced with enthusiasm the idea that wearing a veil was a question of making an existential political decision. The most spectacular intervention of this kind was by Jack Straw. He said that when a veiled Muslim constituent comes to his surgery, he asks her to remove it. In a great example of irony - of which he was possibly unaware - we had a man in a position of power asking for a woman to remove an item of her clothing in the name of greater power to the women's movement. Little wonder the Fawcett Society were moved to comment, "The furore around the veil was typical of how we mistreat ethnic minority women in Britain. It was striking how in the discussion of an issue raised by one of the most powerful white men in the country, Muslim women remained practically voiceless".

His comments sparked a minor rush, with several ministers, including Tony Blair himself, describing the veil as, in one form or another, an unhealthy symbol of cultural separation. For the Opposition, David Davis used the occasion to remark that many Muslims were desiring "voluntary apartheid".

They were comments barely possible from the political mainstream in the past. Indeed, it was precisely on these grounds that many in the left of centre welcomed them; for example Prospect editor David Goodhart, who says "it's part of challenging things that a while ago would have been considered taboo by the media class: the gap between what ordinary people say and what the political and media class say had grown too wide and in the past 2 years its narrowed." There is evidence however that this taboo-breaking is helping to shape rather than just reflect public attitudes; an ICM poll for the BBC in November showed that a third of people now support legislation to ban veil-wearing in public places.

One of the clear legacies of 2006 therefore was to defamiliarise the veil, to make noteworthy, even weird or dangerous, something which had hitherto been as unremarkable as a nun's habit, or the attire of an ultra Orthodox Jew.

The international context is crucial. The veil debate is a Europe-wide one, and one which Britain entered quite late. France, Germany, Italy and Belgium have all enacted legislation, at a national or federal level, curtailing the wearing of some Islamic clothing by women. Unlike Britain, these countries often have explicit legal or constitutional elevation for secularism. Most dramatic of all, perhaps, and most ironically given its reputation for social liberalism is the Netherlands, which is introducing a ban on the wearing of the burqa in public, largely at the instigation of the country's immigration minister Rita Verdonk. In the Netherlands, it's reported that only a few dozen women actually wear the burqa. Similarly in the UK, it is reported that only a very small minority of Muslim women wear the veil.

The debate clearly therefore derives its impact at a symbolic rather than immediately practical level. The veil debate is part of a general moral panic about Muslims within secular states. It is one, among a range of issues, where Muslims and their active presence within a population, apparently pose a challenge - to variously - public safety, secularism, Enlightenment values and Christian traditions (e.g. the spate of stories in December 2006 suggesting that public expression of Christmas was to be inhibited because of "politically correct" sensitivities over Muslim aggression).

It's important to resolve this issue and it's important to work out whether or not it's problematic to be a practising Muslim in a secular state. This is vital firstly because an effective foreign policy, especially if it has an ethical dimension, needs to be clear about what constitutes British values. And it's also important for instrumentalist reasons – the stance of the secular West with regard to the outward manifestations of Islam has a big impact on tendencies within the Muslim world itself.

The way things were going in 2006, it was beginning to look like that issue will indeed be resolved and will see Britain decide that a secular society is indeed inconsistent with outward manifestations of Islam. But those who espouse a coherent, effective and progressive foreign policy should surely be in the vanguard of tackling Islamaphobia in Britain and Europe. That's one reason why it was so depressing that the most prominent minister to take up the veils issue, Jack Straw, had so recently been Foreign Secretary. The great challenge is to establish an overriding principle, that a secular state can happily contain within itself the outward manifestations of all religions, from Islam to Scientology, consistent with the law. The moment ministers start conceding that there is indeed a problem with one public aspect of religion they are confirming the essential point made by theocrats: that Islam does indeed occupy a unique place when it comes to accommodation with the West. That has a big impact domestically, in increasing Muslim feelings of victimhood (cynically stoked up, of course, by several activist groups). One paradoxical effect is that the thousands of British Muslim women who every year cast off the veil will now find it more difficult to do so, as their ability to exercise that choice will have been constrained by a politicisation of that choice. Needless to say, this domestic division, and the security concerns which it produces, may - certainly in the post-Blair world - have an impact on a government's ability to exercise UK foreign policy freely.

There is a powerful global dimension to this, too. All over the Muslim world there are women's movements of one kind or another. It is futile to pretend that these are making great strides;

if anything, from Iraq to Lebanon the truth is in the opposite direction. Nevertheless, in every Muslim country there are, under varying circumstances, women who are in public life, and opposing the power of theocrats. Though their circumstances vary wildly, all of these women share the fact that their feminism takes place within the embrace of Islam, not outside it. Interpretations of Islam which suggest the religion is itself unreformably antipathetic to women's rights, e.g. from Irshad Manji or Ayaan Hirsi Ali are of no practical use at all to women in Muslim countries. Political postures from Western politicians which appear to agree with this sentiment e.g. from European politicians on the veil issue are worse than useless, for they reinforce the idea internationally that Islam and womens' rights, and therefore secular life in general, are irreconcilable.

Maleiha Malik of King's College London says the veil debate "actually plays into the hands of those people that want to argue the model for liberal democracy aren't appropriate for Muslim countries… Whereas an argument that shows that Muslim culture and Liberal democracies are compatible, is going to be a lot more helpful to women feminists in those sorts of countries." And Mandana Hendessi of the Women's National Commission explained that she had already noticed a "fear from women in Middle East about how they view us in Europe. I've seen many Muslim Women's Associations in Egypt that have shown anger at how women in Europe have been treated and in response there has been a reaction, noticeably a more radicalised movement towards political Islam."

Paradoxically perhaps, the situation in the United States is considerably less inflammatory as far as the veil is concerned. American Islamic feminist Asra Nomani confirms that the debate is much less fierce than in Europe; in the U.S the debate over foreign policy, intense and at times Islamaphobic though that is, is almost entirely decoupled from the series of sociological challenges to the country's own Muslim population along the lines we have seen in Europe. On this subject at least, the U.K should move closer to the U.S and away from the wretched example set by continental Europe.

As a British Muslim there was always one certainty - that Labour ministers would pay lip service at least to the ideals of multiculturalism. The world needs more, not less, multiculturalism; Labour ministers have turned their backs on that commitment at the worst possible time.

Urmee Khan is the Commissioning Editor, Features for The Guardian's G2 Supplement. She has written extensively on multiculturalism and being a Muslim in Britain.

Religion, Development and Foreign Policy

Dr Daleep Mukarji

Faith in the public arena has become a new and important issue, particularly post 9/11 and the New York attacks. Today we hear people speak of the clash of civilisations, the fight between Christianity and Islam and the fears in Europe because of new immigrant communities with different cultures, religions and lifestyles. Yet religion has never really left the public space – even in a more modern and secular world. It is here to stay in all societies. Faith and foreign policy issues may appear a new concept. Yet from the days of the crusades, to colonisation, the cold war, and now with the language and agenda of the US administration, faith issues have often motivated or influenced the way nations have interacted with each other.

International development, as a formal objective of governments, global institutes like the UN, World Bank and the IMF, and of secular and faith-based aid agencies, is essentially a post-Second World War phenomenon. Aid and foreign policy were often linked with the overseas development departments as part of the foreign ministries. Many European and North American churches and the wider public have formed special agencies to respond to need, particularly in developing countries in the context of refugees, war, famine, floods, poverty and the provision of basic health and educational services. Thus secular and faith-based aid agencies became very much a part of the public response to need overseas. They have been inspired by a basic principle to help people in need – to love your neighbour.

The dream of the international community in the post war development decades was to use aid to help countries and people to come out of poverty. This approach of governments, the international institutes and aid agencies, while well intentioned, did not often look at the root causes of poverty, inequality, discrimination and marginalisation. There were local factors in the culture, religion and power relations that contributed to poverty and there were also world wide structural and economic reasons why countries and people stayed poor. This understanding has led to the education, organisation, mobilisation and empowerment of people and nations to challenge structures and systems that keep people poor. Such a desire has been part of the inspiration and aspiration of recent movements like Jubilee 2000 for debt relief, the Trade Justice Movement and the Make Poverty History campaign. Often people of faith have led such movements and shown that communities across faiths (and those with none) could influence the overseas policies of governments in the G8, Europe, WTO, the World Bank, IMF and the UN.

Ordinary people want a greater say in foreign policy – not just to leave it to governments, politicians, diplomats and the establishment elite. They want a more ethical foreign policy and one that can help build a just, inclusive, sustainable and safer world community. All faiths speak of care for the weak and vulnerable and doing good, of seeking peace and resolving differences. Sadly also many of the problems within nations and between nations have religious dimensions. Fundamentalists of all religions, or people who feel they are right (and therefore others wrong) because they have either been chosen or instructed by "God" to control, hurt or eliminate others, can show how religion can be used as a powerful force for doing harm.

Challenges in Religion and Development – some issues faced by aid agencies

(a) **The Global War on Terror**

Since 9/11 and the terrorist attacks in Madrid, London, South and South East Asia, there is a growing sense that human and national security must be protected. This is necessary – but the international community must ensure that this so called war on terrorism does not become a war between Christians and Muslims. Human security for people of North America and Europe seems to be the essence of this war. Yet what about the lives, livelihoods and basic survival of people and nations in the South or developing countries? Here one child dies every 3 seconds, 1.2 billion people live below the poverty line (£0.60 per person per day), 800 million go hungry every day, and HIV/AIDS kills 600 people every day in South Africa. Disease, poverty and the lack of resources kills far too many people too early. Much of this is preventable. Surely some of the resources for the global war on terrorism could be set aside for a war on poverty and discrimination? At the same time we need to study in each case – why are people choosing violence to have their say? Foreign policy in the UK and USA may contribute to the alienation and violence we see amongst a few young Muslims.

(b) Conflicts, wars and ethnic strife

Unfortunately many of the areas of major conflicts today are places where there are religious and ethnic tensions – Israel and the Occupied Palestinian Territories, Sudan, Sri Lanka, India and Pakistan, Ethiopia/Somalia, etc. In such situations humanitarian agencies try to provide relief and alleviate suffering. They can be accused of taking sides, of being biased as they look at the root causes and sadly in many such places it is extremely risky for aid agency staff. In Sri Lanka, Afghanistan and Sudan some have lost their lives. Here again global institutions have a vital role for a just peace, for peace keeping and conflict resolution. It also needs dialogue, trust and confidence building mechanisms across communities of faith at the grass root level as Christian Aid is doing in Sierra Leone, the DRC, Northern Nigeria, Sri Lanka and the Middle East through its partners.

(c) The place of faith based organisations

In countries of the North where many faith based agencies are raising resources to support relief and development there are suspicions about the agenda and use of these funds. Will this money be used only to help one faith community, will it be used to convert others, or will it be used to "support terrorism"? These are genuine concerns. Agencies who are signatories to the International Code of Conduct for Humanitarian Relief (Red Cross Code) sign up to help people in need irrespective of religion or race and would not use funds in any way to proselytise. They are also expected to be open and accountable about the use of their funds.

Christian Aid is a Christian agency and proud of its Christian heritage, identity, name and faith based status. "Christian" (in Christian Aid) says why we do international development. We want to assist people and to be prophetic – to speak out when we see injustice, poverty and exclusion. We are willing to take sides with poor people and enable them to have a voice and influence in the international scene. "Christian" is our inspiration and "Aid" is what we do with and through partners in over 50 countries. This policy to help people in need irrespective of their faith or ethnicity is central to our approach. It is certainly the approach of all agencies who are members of the Disasters Emergency Committee (DEC/UK) and who have signed up to the code.

Some faith based agencies, particularly Muslim ones, are always under suspicion. What is their agenda and are they helping groups who promote violence? One or two have been investigated. All faith based groups are accountable to the Charity Commission, the public, and to governments for funds and activities. Yet new laws and practices of certain institutions or governments continue to imply that for some of us all may not be above board or transparent. These concerns should not victimise Islamic charities.

In many countries, faith based organisations are probably the most vibrant parts of civil society. This is certainly true of Africa and South Asia where much of the world's poverty is located. Without the involvement of local faith leaders and their communities it would be difficult to deal with HIV/AIDS and other problems. The international aid community (both Governments and aid agencies) will need to consider seriously how to fund and use these local faith communities in long term development.

(d) Faith and development issues

More recently, the US government, heavily influenced by US Christian evangelicals, has cut off aid to UN agencies that in any way promoted reproductive rights, family planning, or provided training/support for abortions. They have also put conditions on their HIV/AIDS funding – to promote abstention, oppose sex education and condemn the use of condoms. This has been very difficult for many African countries where the problem of HIV/AIDS is an every day disaster for families and communities. Sometimes US Government policies exclude working with local sex workers thus depriving local development agencies from a very direct entry point into addressing the issue of HIV/AIDS. At UN conferences it is unusual to see the US Government, the Vatican and Muslim countries come together to oppose some aspects of gender equality and basic human rights for people if it challenges their faith or cultural perspective.

Such views that influence funding, aid policies and alliances with various governments have brought a new dimension to religion as it influences the aid and foreign policy agenda of governments. When it is the US, how aid is perceived and funded does have wider implications.

Religion and Development

In a recent poll in the UK, more people in Britain thought religion causes harm than believed it can do good. An overwhelming majority see religion as a cause of division and tension – 82% say faith causes problems in a country where two thirds say they are not religious (Guardian 23/12/06). The phenomenon of violence, conflicts and international disputes in the early 21st century shows how complex relations between communities and nations are. It is also a challenge and opportunity for faiths to be agents for change, for good and for peace and harmony. This will mean working together to influence both world leaders but also grass root groups who may see violence as the only way to solve some of their problems. Underpinning much of this tension are the issues of power, of justice and of poverty. People in the developing world experience the destruction of their communities either by local leaders or by the persistence of a new global power group – of the rich nations and multinational companies – who use military, economic, cultural and political means to dominate others. In this context religion and culture have been both a source of oppression and liberation.

In 2007, Britain is celebrating 200 years of the start of the abolition of slavery with the passing of a bill in parliament in 1807. It was a religious and political leader, working with others, William Wilberforce, who showed that this treatment of others could be changed. It influenced policy in the UK and the colonies. In the late eighteenth century this was a major movement – to stop slavery.

We are now living in a very plural, multicultural, multiethnic and multi-faith world. Foreign and national policies will need to recognise this reality and with it the need for multilateral solutions to many of the world's problems. In this context the role and potential of the UN in global governance and the multilateral talks on trade (WTO), Climate Change (the post Kyoto options) and peaceful solutions to some of the conflicts, particularly in the wider Middle East will need dialogue across faiths, races and power groups.

The challenge of the 21st century is to see how we can build institutes and relationships across nations that can make it safer for people and the planet. In this process religion and religious people can be very much part of the solution. We need a modern secular state that gives space and opportunity for people to practice their faith and avoids clashes or rivalries between faiths. This will need politicians, religious leaders and the wider community to work together. Religion is only one aspect of the complex reality where people and nations, who for years have felt excluded or oppressed are now trying to claim space and voice for their identity, their culture and their values. They want "justice" and equality. In nations of the global south, faith is being used by politicians to take power, create a national identity and form alliances across nations and ethnic groups.

Aid agencies, international institutions and both foreign and domestic policies of all nations will need to come to terms with this changing reality. It is one world and one human race – but we cannot ignore the diversity of religion, culture and ethnicity. Religion will be a major reality in society in the years ahead – and one that will need to be dealt with within the context of any ethical and enlightened domestic and foreign policy agenda.

Dr Daleep Mukarji has been the Director of Christian Aid since 1998. Born in India, he previously worked as a doctor, becoming general secretary of the Christian Medical Association of India. He was formerly Executive Secretary for Health, Community and Justice at the World Council of Churches in Geneva.

About the Foreign Policy Centre

The Foreign Policy Centre is a leading European think tank launched under the patronage of the British Prime Minister Tony Blair to develop a vision of a fair and rule-based world order. We develop and disseminate innovative policy ideas which promote:

- Effective multilateral solutions to global problems
- Democratic and well-governed states as the foundation of order and development
- Partnerships with the private sector to deliver public goods
- Support for progressive policy through effective public diplomacy
- Inclusive definitions of citizenship to underpin internationalist policies

The Foreign Policy Centre has produced a range of seminal publications by key thinkers on subjects ranging from the future of Europe and international security to identity and the role of non-state actors in policymaking. They include *A Global Alliance for Global Values* by Tony Blair, *After Multiculturalism* by Yasmin Alibhai-Brown, *The Post-Modern State and the World Order* by Robert Cooper, *Network Europe* and *Public Diplomacy* by Mark Leonard, *The Beijing Consensus* by Joshua Cooper Ramo, *Trading Identities* by Wally Olins and *Pre-empting Nuclear Terrorism* by Amitai Etzioni.

The Centre runs a rich and varied events programme which allows people from business, government, NGOs, think-tanks, lobby groups and academia to interact with speakers who include Prime Ministers, Presidents, Nobel Prize laureates, global corporate leaders, activists, media executives and cultural entrepreneurs from around the world. For more information, please visit www.fpc.org.uk